A Divine Walk
Through My Soul

I0176824

Poetry and Quotes Envisioned By
Lourdes Alexander

Published by True Beginnings Publishing. Copyright Lourdes Alexander, 2019.

Formatting, Editing, and all artwork by True Beginnings Publishing. All Illustrations, Cover Art, and text are Copyright Protected.

ISBN-13: 978-1-947082-84-7
ISBN-10: 1-947082-84-1

Ordering Information:
To order additional copies of this book, please visit Amazon or the Author's website at: https://www.lourdesalexander.com/

Reviews

"How should I express my boundless gratitude to internet technology for bestowing me a lot of literary and invaluable friends on the Facebook all over India as well as abroad?

Dear Lourdes Alexander is the most invaluable of them. Since my student life, I've been a voracious reader and have read most of the Hindi, Urdu and English poets, writers, journalists, critics and columnist. It was the year 2014, a significant year of my life, when I had a rare opportunity to come across the poetess Lourdes Alexander from the most glamorous city of India, MUMBAI, on the Facebook. Since then, no day has passed without reading her creations. Her poetry and quotes are extremely inspiring, romantic, and full of the passions of love. Undoubtedly, her creations touch the core of the reader's heart. I've enjoyed her plentiful creations so far. The way of her expression, choosing unusual themes and beautiful texture of her words make her extraordinary and a popular poetess in the world of English Literature. Going through her creations, I wonder how many years ago the emotions of her heart started to get beautiful shapes through her ink. Even she herself couldn't have learnt when the seeds of poetry had grown up in the fertile soil of her tender heart and branched out in the form of a huge tree. For a long time, this tree of poetry has been providing cool shade to the pedestrians who are on the way to the destination of human life. Fortunate are those who get an opportunity to read her. One of the distinguished features of her writing is that the reader can easily feel the intensity of her emotions appropriately, and it becomes very difficult for the reader to quit before the complete reading of her creations. The words emerging from her Divine Soul are really most appealing and unforgettable. The poetess holds the readers in the grip of her ink, unbreakingly. Sometimes, her creations make me feel how much sorrows, pains, and agonies she has hidden in the cell of her heart. What a miraculous management of DESTINY it is! Quite unknown hearts come across on the way to the destination of human life. At this early stage of her life, the poetess is casting unending spell of her poetry over millions of readers. After going through her creations, readers feel that an indelible mark of her beautiful poetry has been marked on their memory screens.

Wishing her a glorious life. May Lord Jesus bless her boundlessly!"
~Madan Vaishnava "Shakunta," Retd. Professor in English,
BEAWAR, District AJMER, Rajasthan, India

"I enjoy Lourdes' poetry. I have made time over the past two years to follow and share her writings. I find them to be stimulating, inspiring, and worth following..."
~Sarah Anne, West Alexandria, Ohio, USA

"The writings of Lourdes knocks directly on the heart of the reader and binds him emotionally to the feelings expressed, while making him visually capable to see things in the imagination."
~Saumendra Nayak (Author), Mumbai, India

"I have long been following Lourdes Alexander's posts on Facebook and have found her work uplifting and inspirational. I am looking forward to reading more in the future, and particularly in a published format."
~Gerald R. Wright (Author), Torrevieja, Spain

"I've never considered myself a romantic. Always figured love is love, and that's it, until I discovered the writings of Lourdes Alexander. Found her writings by accident which ultimately expressed my true feelings about love, feelings, and spiritual connection. Until then, I had never found anyone's writings that even came close to expressing my true feelings, which left me amazed. Of course, there's plenty of flowery prose available, but none relatable until I discovered her writings. Here's a young woman who has summed up my feelings about love, connections, and beliefs in her writings that can only come from her heart and soul. Writings I not only relate to, but find solace, comfort, and a connection in. Lourdes Alexander has the ability to appeal to your inner most thoughts and beliefs, feelings you may not be in touch with. And for those of you who are skeptical, don't think her writings would appeal to you, read at least a few samples and I'm convinced that you as I will discover how Lourdes will appeal to the most hardened of hearts."
~Henry Coe, The Villages, Florida, USA

"Lourdes is a talented lady who gets to the heart of the matter in all that she writes. I am looking forward to seeing more of her wonderful work."
~Allen Baswell (Journalist/Writer), Ackerman ,Mississippi, USA

"... there are many ways to express the heart, and she does it in words, the hardest of the arts... just perfect."
~Rolf R. Rohn, Pittsburgh, Pennsylvania, USA

"Lourdes has soul-deep expression to her words, and in those words her beauty shines with dazzling brilliance."
~Lawrence Parent, Hayward, Wisconsin, USA

"Lourdes ma'am is a renowned poetess whose poetry goes straight into the heart, and it's got the sensibility to grab the attention of readers. I love the way she pens down her deepest emotions in a lucid style. May God bless her, always."
~Spoorthy Sharone, Vijayawada, India

"A very loving poet with talent and feelings in her poetry! Her writings touch the souls and spirits of her diverse readers."
~Rose Huy Woolket, Walnut Creek, California, USA

"Lourdes Alexander is an undiscovered talent who writes from the heart, her poems reflect her life's journey as she opens up her feelings her beliefs and especially her heart and exposes the workings of a beautiful mind. I have been impressed with Lourdes poetry over the past few years, and it's time for her poems to be seen by a wider audience and I wish her every success with her future books."
~Paul Griffiths, Birkenhead, UK

"Lourdes Alexander perpetually excels in her writings. Her new book isn't just another book filled with poems and quotes. It's a gorgeous, hard-to-categorize series of reflections themed around love, life, and spirituality that also portrays what it means to remember those who we've lost."

~Rohit Rajani, Mumbai, India

"Lourdes pours her heart and soul into her writing, striking a chord of relateability with others. Hopefully, she continues writing, and I look forward to what's in store."

~Scott Thomas Meyers (Author), Newport, NH, USA

"Lourdes Alexander began swapping verse with me a few years ago in my Facebook poetry group, The Poetry Group. I soon learned that Lourdes writes from a cavernous garret, deep within her heart... and from the essence of divinity that is the light of her soul's path. What you read, is what you get... no smokescreens here. Lourdes lays it all out for your perusal, and hopefully your inspiration!

~Ricky Cochran (Author), Pittsburgh, PA, USA

"Lourdes writes from a place that you can only find deep within yourself. She has felt a love for another human being that did not show her the same emotions. Her words show great love and admiration that only a women who has felt the deepest of love and pangs of pain can express. Sometimes, you get confused in her poetry, but I think she wants you to so you can feel the same way that she does or has in her life. What is love without all of those factors intertwined?"

~Bathsheba Dailey (Author), Buffalo, WV, USA

Table of Contents

Poems

Quotes

This book is Dedicated to...
My Loving Sister.

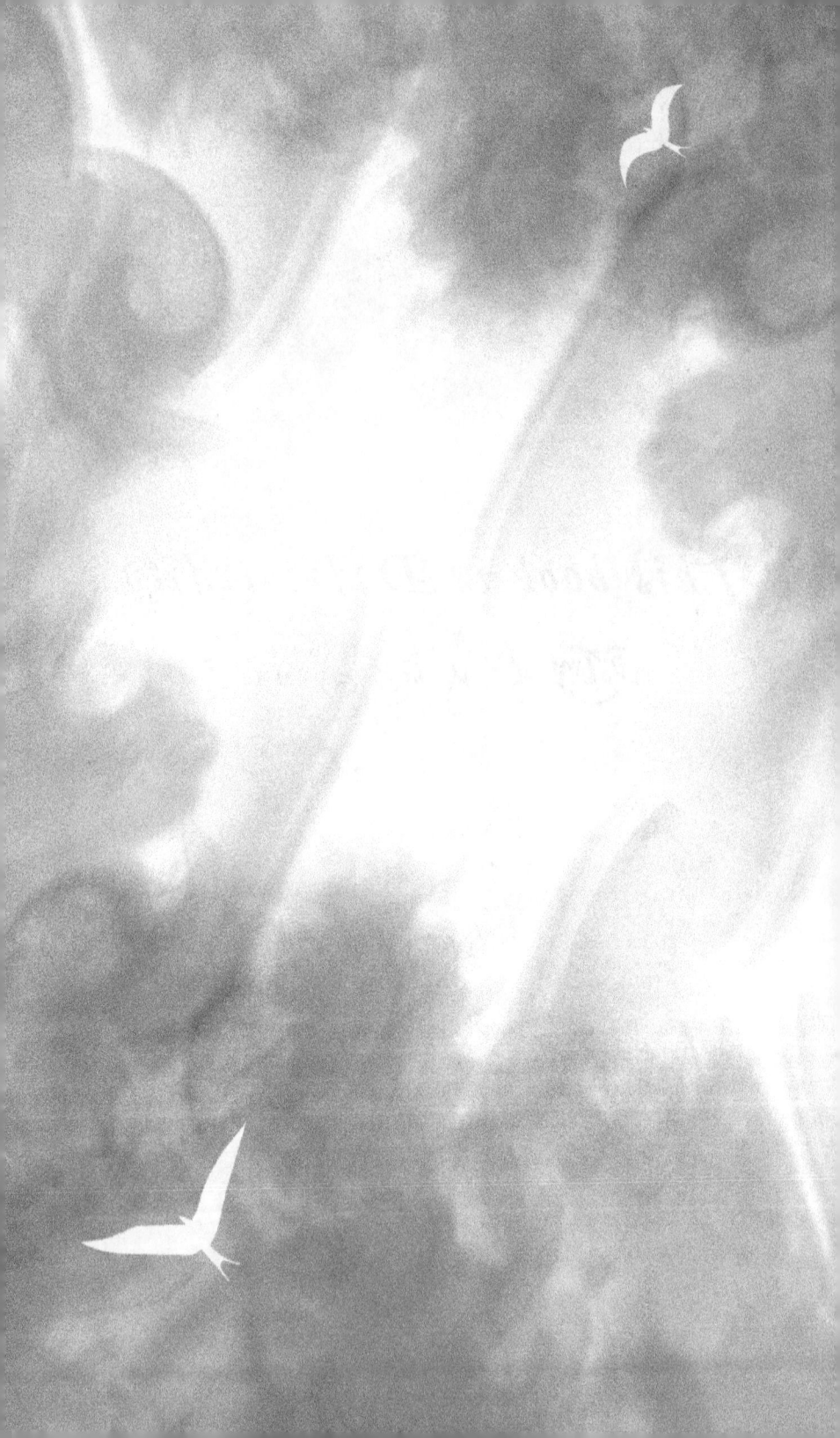

Poetry

Lourdes Alexander

A Poem for Sophia

My darling and loving little sis,
It is you I truly miss.
You'll never know your passing left such a space
That nothing in this world could ever replace...

I cherish every moment we shared together.
I never had such joy, since, from any other.
When you left me, it broke my heart.
Your passing blew my world apart...

The hurt I feel inside, you will never know.
As your big sister, I watched you grow.
I still recall those childish pranks we used to do.
Nobody ever made me laugh as much as you...

No one else will ever understand
The bond of love we shared just by holding hands.
We even used to argue, and we'd often fight,
But we always kissed and made up at the end of the night...

I remember the way we would go out and shop,
Walking all over the town until we dropped.
We shared our clothes, we brushed each other's hair.
You'd kiss me on my forehead to show you cared...

Whenever my confidence failed, or I felt down,
I always felt better knowing you were around.
Your smile picked me up when all else failed.
You were my emotional lifeboat, my guiding sail...

Sometimes I treated you as if you were my daughter,
Mothering you with love, taking you out of troubled waters.
You often acted stupid, playing up and being wild.
When I lost you, it felt like I'd lost my own child...

I can never forget that terrible day,
When the hand of fate snatched you away.
That memory still shakes me to my core,
Knowing I will never get to see you anymore...

I often cry when I think of you.
Then my tears start falling, and I don't know what to do.
If I could be granted a wish, I'd wish for you,
But I know such a wish can never come true...

Only the good Lord above knows the reason why
This was your chosen time to die.
But I know that He knows best.
That's why He called you to eternal rest...

So, my darling little sister, I will not complain,
For I know in Heaven we shall meet again,
To do all those things that loving sisters do.
But, until that day, my poem is for you...

Will You Hold Me Close

Will you hold me close and keep me safe?
Wrap me up in your gentle embrace?
I can feel your love when we're apart.
Can I be the one to rent out your heart?
I only have to look into your eyes to know you will.
Your words reassure my soul and make me be still.
You calm the raging storm that surrounds me.
Now my broken wings are healed, so I can fly free.
My belief in you grows stronger by the day.
How is it that you make me feel this way?
Your faith penetrates deep into the very soul of me.
When you look into my eyes, please tell me what you see.
My world was broken and falling apart.
Now I feel your love with every beat of my heart.
I don't know how this happened, but it is meant to be;
That you will always be with me...

No Distance At All

He loved her so much,
His greatest fear was to lose her.
Time is such a fleeting thing
As it slipped through his fingers like falling sand.
He couldn't function without her, he wanted her,
Needed her to be his.
Theirs was a distant love,
A hope built upon a shared dream.
He wanted to express his love for her in words,
Words of love he would trace all over her body
To make her feel his love crossed distant oceans.
This was a love she had never experienced.
She felt wanted and alive again.
The fire of desire burned as one flame.
She felt wanted by his need,
Rediscovering her smile long since lost.
Had Destiny pulled them together for a lifetime,
A dream of the reality of their dream?
Had he seen her in another life, another time,
Knowing her without knowing her?
He knew the touch of her skin before holding her,
The fragrance of her body without smelling her scent,
The sweetness of her lips without even a kiss.
She sensed this in him and found herself through him.
Theirs was a love that had crossed over the void,
A connection, a bond that had tethered their souls,
Intimate beyond the realms of physical intimacy.
He felt her, sensed her, knew what she was thinking,
Just as she gave him answers to questions yet to be asked.
He wanted to sweep her off her feet, to dance a dance of love.

She wanted to be held close and melt into his warm embrace.
They wanted to be wanted by only each other,
To walk on life's path and together hold hands.
Would fate be kind and bring them together,
Or would fate be cruel and tear their hearts apart?
She had a secret in the form of an illness.
When she finally told him, he told her he knew.
This made her smile, and she smiled just for him...

Love Is Blind

He loved her with a passion.
For her, he would give anything.
She was his everything, she was his world,
He was willing to lose it all.
Without her, nothing seemed to matter.
She had taught him the meaning of life;
That life was worth living.
She made him see the beauty of life like never before,
Yet she could not see such things; she was blind,
But she did not want to be pitied — she wanted to be loved.
Even her blindness couldn't stop her living life to the fullest.
He realized she faced this dark storm alone, fearlessly.
It made him feel ashamed of feeling sorry for himself.
It was time to lick clean his wounded pride.
He had long forgotten the essence of life,
More robot now than human, an emotionless shell,
But now he had a mission to make her see again,
So he bartered his life against the price of her treatment.
He was a fighter, a boxer by profession,
But for her he would take a dive
To lose a fight as she battled for sight.
He knew the big money men would kill him for this,
But she was worth dying for.
He took the dive because he fell in love.
Beaten so badly, he was left in a coma,
Lying alone in his hospital bed,
Trapped in his own darkness.

She now had the gift of sight, living her dream as a nurse.
Months passed by, she never knew the man in the coma
Or that he sacrificed it all for her,
But she felt drawn to him as he silently slept.
She somehow knew him, but didn't.
He was so close to his love, but now he could not see her.
As time moved on, she would sit at his bedside reading him poetry.
Somehow, by some chance, her words of love touched him.
He opened his eyes.
Hers was the first face he saw, the face of an angel.
They looked into each other's eyes and just knew.
They knew they were drawn together by fate.
He smiled and said, "You can see me!"
She laughed. "Yes, of course I can! Have we met before?"
"Yes," he said, "but in another time when you were in a darker place."
It was then she knew what love really was.
For the first time, they both could see...

Fooled By Love

You were my destiny,
A heaven-sent blessing, I believed.
I looked upon you as an Angel,
Surrendered my heart, mind, and soul.
I believed every word you said.
I emptied myself freely for your sake.
Little did I know, I was a fool for love.
You never treasured me like you did when you touched my soul.
You showed the other side of you
That made my heart crack into pieces.
You once had lifted my spirit.
You crushed my self-respect and stole my confidence from me.
My heart and soul not only ached in pain,
I wept so much that my tears have run dry.
They stopped to flow as they whispered, "It was all in vain."
You were the one who helped me to gather the pieces of my heart.
Never dreamed in my wildest dream
You would become the reason to break it once again.
I'd have carried on life's journey even if you'd turned into a beast.
I did not deserve such pain for loving you.
A trust I gave, my trust betrayed,
Now I have lost my faith in love forever...

Whispering My Love

Can you hear the soft whisper of love,
Softly and tenderly falling on your ears?
Does it need to shout,
Or can you hear the soft whisper?
Ask me if you have any doubt...

Some say love is blind.
It can happen overnight.
I don't know when this feeling grew.
I don't know how to convince you.
I don't know if you will understand.
Without meeting, I have fallen for you...

Love doesn't need a physical presence.
Love can happen in an instant,
For I believe love's touch is pure and divine.
It can grow even without looking into each other's eyes...

It was your care and concern
That broke the walls that were frozen,
Releasing me from my own prison
And leading me to you
Without any personal gratification...

Do you feel the same for me,
For I can hear love's sweet whisper clearly?
It makes me blush.
It makes me cry.
I must admit, I cannot lie...

I wish this distance would slowly fade.
I wish I had wings,
Then I don't need to board a jet plane.
So, whenever you hear sweet whispers in your ears,
Remember it's me thinking of you, my dear...

Finding New Hope

She can hear the sound of wind chimes
As they hang upon the porch.
She listens to the ticking of the old clock,
The sound of children's laughter, echoes from the playground,
Though she can't see what is happening around her...

Her head is hurting, she feels almost blindfolded
As the darkness slowly envelopes each day.
Every time she tries to rise, she almost collapses.
The light in her eyes slowly fades, draining the radiance from her eyes...

She has so much to do, yet so little time;
A book to write, pictures to paint,
A life to live, a love to find.
This is a process of cleaning...

But there is no life left in her
As she battles her own self-doubt.
Can she overcome this battle?
She will survive, she was born to fight...

Words Of Love

She talked to him through her poetry,
For she was very shy.
He visualized the words and understood what she never said,
Though she sometimes told him little white lies,
For he read everything between the lines...
Their love so distant, yet so close,
Poetry transcended all barrier between them.
Their soul had unknowingly connected
As in each other's dreams they met.
Their days passed with greetings of good morning and goodnight,
Though in different time zones they lived.
Yet their hearts crossed all boundaries,
Conquering even space and time.
They both blushed crimson when thoughts crossed their mind.
Love's touch had made them dreamers in their own world.
A hope kept flickering.
Someday, they will unite
As they lived and dreamed beneath the same sky...

His Rose

She was his delicate rose,
Born amidst sharp thorns.
He called her his muse,
The one who had transformed him
From a heartless beast into a man,
For she inspired him
To write love sonnets...

His love story didn't seem
To have a happy ending,
For she lay on her sickbed,
Fragile, pale, weary, and weak,
With no trace of smile or radiance.
He felt her room was filled with darkness,
As if the angel of Death hovered around
While she lay comatose, peacefully,
Like a sleeping beauty...

The thought of losing her
Made him numb and emotionally paralyzed.
He wanted to take away all her aches and pain,
But all his efforts went in vain.
He even went on his knees and prayed,
Pleading to the Divine
To take his life instead,
For she was his breath
And life without her
Would not be the same...

He had read the story
Of the Sleeping Beauty
Coming to life with her lover's kiss.
So, he wondered to himself
If his love had the power
To break the spell of death.
So, he leaned and kissed his ladylove on her lips, passionately,
And waited for her to open her eyes, immediately,
But when she didn't make any move,
He looked at the heavens and cried frantically like a baby...

He couldn't break the spell.
His love wasn't true, he felt.
God couldn't see his tears,
So He breathed life into her.
Suddenly, he saw her open her eyes,
Witnessing a miracle,
Realizing love's touch indeed had the power
To bring a dead person back to life...

Breaking The Silence

She lay on the bed,
Trying to sleep.
She knew her body
Needed to be healed,
But her mind kept wandering
With fears that held her captive.
Even the creased sheets caused her discomfort,
So she kept changing sides,
Trying to drift to sleep.
That's when words began to pour out,
Without any restraint like a dam.
She jotted down before it vanished from her mind,
For she was a poet
Whose mind was never still.
She had used it enough,
And her pen always needed to be refilled.
She loved this breakthrough
In her imaginary world,
For she slowly discovered her true self.
No one disturbed her.
No one rejected her,
And she never fumbled,
Nor felt shy or inferior.
It was through words
She broke her silence...

Discovering Love

Let me lay on your bare chest.
Caress me like no one has caressed me ever before.
Trace your emotions with your fingers all over me,
And I will read them back to you.
Rub your feet against mine.
Hug me tight.
Let our bodies intertwine.
Kiss me in a way
That I would cry with joy,
Feeling blessed to have you in my life.
Make me feel wanted, my love.
Show me your soul had been desperately searching
For a twin flame,
And can't spend this life's journey alone.
Let your love rain over me,
A parched heart so long it had been,
A desert without a bloom,
Frozen on a wintry night,
Afraid of falling in love,
For my heart wasn't handled right.
Heal the scars that're still wounded
With your gentle and magical touch.
Don't stop if you hear me whimper,
'Cause I would be rejoicing for being loved.
Feed my soul with your passion.
Let me taste your mind,
Your secret desires,
For I know this is sex for the soul that we both seek,
Pure love so sublime...

Slow Dance

He watched her,
Knowing she felt lost among the crowd.
He felt like something was holding her back.
She needed to be comforted.
He walked up to her,
Held her hand,
And led her to the dance floor.
As the orchestra played a romantic song,
He pulled her in close to him.
He was mesmerized by the aroma of her perfume.
The scent of romance hung in the air.
Leaning in, he bent to kiss her lips.
She melted in his arms
Like a candle.
She felt safe in his arms.
An instant glow appeared on her face.
She became vibrant and lively, like a spring leaf.
The eyes that once seemed drained now shined.
They radiated with love
She felt saved; he had rescued her heart,
Now she could begin to live again...

Moments Like These

From my window I can see it's snowing.
I warm my hands by the fireplace
As the cold wind howls outside.
I need to snuggle into you,
All warm and cozy.
Oh, how I miss you in moments like these
As I travel down memory lane,
Reminded of days gone by
When we used to throw snowballs at each other.
I remember the sleigh rides as if they were yesterday.
Will we do those things again?
Can those good old days ever return...?

Love Sealed

Words can't express the measure of my love,
For each sunrise and sunset belongs to you.
Lost in a world of fantasy,
Where you and I only dwell,
Nothing attracts me now
As my soul desires to be with you.
Every time I stare at you,
Your eyes speak a thousand words,
Testifying to me
How deep your love is;
Deeper than the sea,
Two bodies though we are,
But bound as one soul,
For our love doesn't need
Any stamp paper to seal our love...

The Love I Need

All I seem to have are words,
I have had them so often thrown at me.
Words have hurt me in the past,
But, maybe, someday, one day,
Tomorrow will be our day.
Words for me are merely words.
I want to believe that you really love me,
For love is sustained by actions.
Show me what I mean to you.
I am not asking you to pluck the stars from the sky.
They look perfect as a heavenly constellation.
Neither do I need diamonds or pearls.
I have no need for such enticements.
All I need is true love, a lover who cares,
A lover who will share a love that is pure,
Someone to miss me if I'm not there,
A love that would feel dimmed by my absence,
Only to be refreshed by my presence.
That is the kind of love I need,
Something I have longed for,
To be loved not for a day, a month or a year,
But for eternity...

Love Surrounds Me

Love is like a tender breeze,
A dewdrop tear falling from a leaf,
The kiss of the rain as it says hello
To the rising of the morning sun.
Love is the falling white feather off an angel's wing,
That first Valentine's Day card sealed with a kiss,
The sound of church bells ringing on a wedding day,
Clouds in motion drifting in a bright blue sky,
Children's laughter playing happily,
Two lovers walking, holding hands,
Tiny stars that twinkle in the dark night's sky,
And the wing beats of butterflies fluttering by.
It is the songbirds singing the dawn chorus.
Love lies in the beauty that I see before us.
I see it in the early misty morning before it's gone.
Love, it surrounds me, the list goes on.
I can see love all over the place,
But I see real love when I see your smiling face.
Love has a special magic all its own,
For I see love in you, and you alone...

Soulmates

Her heart spoke words of love for him
That her brain could not accept.
She couldn't tell if his soul had connected to hers.
This left her with a strong ache in the depths of her heart.

She was about to bid him adieu and let him go,
Then he gazed into her eyes and it melted her heart.
His love stopped her in her tracks, now she couldn't let him go.
She realized how much she loved him.

Her heart belonged to him,
For this he offered her his soul...

Sharing A Dream

With eyes wide open, she dreamed a dream,
To be his lover, his friend, his all.
He too dreamed a dream and dreamt of her,
But they feared to commit, as life's unfair.
Two bodies entwined in union as one soul,
Beyond the physical touch, their love was on a different plain,
On a higher level of existence.
No distance could distance them,
They only worried about losing each other.
Love is meant to be simple, not complicated or complex.
They would not conform to society's restrictions.
No inhibitions would inhibit their love.
They had decided to walk their own chosen path,
Avoiding the barriers that headed their way.
It was their love for each other that would win the day.
Why worry now about what the future may hold?
They lived in the moment, and the moment felt right,
For they loved each other as only they could.
She trusted him blindly when she looked into his eyes,
For his eyes held a calmness that steadied her soul.
So, she took a step that she was frightened to take,
Knowing the risks and what was at stake.
It was that look in his eyes, a look from her dreams,
For she found her King, and he welcomed his Queen...

All I Ask

Do you miss me?
Will you live your life for me?
Does my absence make you cry?
Do you want to hold me?
Do you miss my kiss,
Tonight and every night...?

Don't speak a word.
Let your love do the talking.
Take me to a place where there is only us,
This magical something
Between you and I.
Love is the only thing I need.
Nothing else matters.
It feeds my soul and makes my day.
Love holds no promises,
But its secrets it keeps,
For love never lies.

I want you to be my rock,
To hold me when things get tough.
In those difficult times when I will need you, my love,
Keep me safe in your arms.
Protect my heart, my soul,
As I will never let you go.

Life can be a bitch at times.
It can make you lose all hope.
Do you understand
Your love will help me withstand,
So I can regain control and take command
Of anything life can throw at me.
Those storms that come our way,
Our love will conquer all.

So, tell me, please,
Do you love me and me alone?
Am I the only one
That you care to care for?
Please, don't ever leave me alone,
Even when things get bad.
Even when I get mad,
Never leave me.

You are my ecstasy,
My soul's elixir.
Show me that you need me,
Let me know you care,
And I will never leave,
I swear...

Entwined In The Rain

As we walk together, hand in hand,
Lost in our own sweet wonderland,
We watch as the clouds gently roll by.
As dark clouds gather up in the sky,
He kisses me and whispers my name.
I kiss him back as it starts to rain.
The sound of thunder fills the air.
He holds me tight, I feel safe without a care.
I kiss him back, he kisses me more,
His love washes over me like a downpour.
When he looks into my eyes, in that moment we realize.
I find myself drowning in his eyes.
This was a perfect moment, like no other,
Standing in the rain with my lover.
In need of shelter, in need of a kiss,
In a downpour of utter bliss,
Romance falls in tiny drops.
I don't want this rain to stop.
It feels so right, like it's meant to be,
Under this heavenly rain, just him and me.
He pulls me close, and he feels fine.
I feel his lips as they touch mine.
His kisses taste as sweet as wine.
We complete each other, I feel it in my soul,
As two halves become a whole.
He whispers he loves me into my ear,
These are the words I have longed to hear.
I am lost in a dream, feels like love is in the air
As he runs his fingers through my wet hair.

I love his touch, it feels sublime.
It sends shivers down my spine.
I feel like singing out his name
To the rhythm of the falling rain.
His touch awakens me so much more.
I feel my skin tingle from every pore.
Lost in the moment, I feel he's mine,
Holding each other, our bodies entwined.
Locked together in a passionate embrace,
I see love when I looks at his face.
Both soaked to the bone, our clothes wet through,
But I felt warm all over because of him.
As we kissed, the sun came out, and the rain was gone,
But the love we felt for each other still lives on.
I always smile whenever it begins to rain.
I relive that perfect moment once again...

His...

She cried, and lied, and then denied
That love mattered to her,
Trying to make herself believe love wasn't meant for her.
It was as if love was playing hide and seek.
She knew it was there somewhere waiting to be found.
Outwardly, she appeared strong, but inside herself she felt weak,
Fearing a life of loneliness, she would break down and weep.
Her tear-stained eyes told him her story that words could not convey.
He could see her like nobody else could.
The look of pain in her tear-stained eyes tore his heart apart.
She saw hope in his smile, a trust beyond promises.
He made her want to come out of her shell.
Like a rose bud she opened up for him,
Showing for the first time her true self.
As he learned more of her, she learned more of him,
He embraced her emotional scars as lessons learnt from life.
As she gave herself over to him, she wept tears of joy.
He smiled and stole a falling tear as if it were a precious jewel.
"I will keep this forever," he said and smiled.
She laughed as she knew her heart belonged to him,
For she knew he was her armor
And would treasure her heart for the rest of his life...

Withered Rose

She decided to get rid of her old books.
Out with the old, in with the new.
As she tossed the books into an old cardboard box,
A withered rose fell from the pages of a book.
Pressed flat and faded, its beauty a victim of time,
But this faded rose brought her a flashback of blissful memories
That tumbled from the bookshelf inside her mind.
As she remembered those happy times with her old love,
The petals of the rose now fell like tears to the floor,
As if it was weeping for that same lost love.
She looked in the mirror and saw a faded rose,
Her beautiful face now aged by the passage of time.
She had lost her bloom.
There was once a love story in her heart,
But now it too was discarded into a cardboard box.
She used to have a life, but now she merely exists.
Her hopes have not died, they only faded away.
She was waiting for that certain someone
To come along and make her smile,
For she was deserving of love,
Waiting in hope to begin another chapter in her book of life.
All she needed was someone to nurture her spirit,
To make her smile so she could bloom again,
And once more become a rose...

Her Loving Touch

When she felt my kick from inside her tummy,
She was overjoyed; I could feel her love before my birth.
I was making my statement clear, I am here!
She never complained about the pain I brought her
As she caressed me gently in her womb and sang to me.
Even before I was born, I knew she was special.
She loved me so much it was like nothing else mattered;
A love unconditional of mother and child.
I became her reason for living, so she could give me life.
Inside her womb, I could feel her sorrow, her worry, her pain.
She loved me even before I was born.
I almost lost her as she gave birth to me.
She nearly died during labor,
But now I was there to see her tear-stained eyes
As they wept for me.
When she saw me for the first time, I watched her smile
As she held me so gently with such tenderness and devotion.
I felt her lips as she kissed my little forehead.
It was her way of showing how much she loved me,
Of how much my arrival on Earth meant to her.
I was her first born.
She carried me patiently inside her for nine long months,
Just to hold me proudly in her loving arms.
Then, she smiled a million-dollar smile,
As if to say, welcome, my child,
To this earthly paradise...

The Hidden Love

He didn't believe in love,
Nor in women.
Love had been playing games;
Cruel and dirty games.
He couldn't discuss with another
How he felt;
Lonely,
Sad,
Dejected,
Miserable.
He couldn't break the silence.
He wanted to live,
To be loved,
To love in return.
His heart was broken
Beyond measure.
He had lost hope in love,
And in life,
Wanted to embrace death,
Put an end to his miserable life.
That's when life took him by surprise.
When she came along in his life,
She could read the pain in his eyes;
A pain which he for so long had hidden.
He pretended all was well,
Was always surrounded by a crowd,
But no one understood that he felt isolated.
She took him by surprise
When she asked him, "What's wrong?
What have you been hiding for so long?
Why are you so sad?
Tell me, I can see it!
Please, don't hide!"

He was taken aback.
How could she know?
She confessed-
"Your eyes already spoke to me.
That love is what you need.
Isn't it true?"
He opened up to her
The things that made him sad.
Slowly, she planted a seed of passion in his heart,
Made him believe that true love indeed existed.
She simply gave him the love that he yearned for;
A true love,
A selfless love,
An unconditional love.
She filled his heart with light.
He began to live.
He felt comforted,
Loved,
And longed for.
She took him out of the shallowness
That was about to drown him.
He wanted to live this life with her.
He loved her.
She loved him.
It wasn't that easy.
They both found a perfect soulmate in each other
But couldn't boldly profess their love to the world.
It was complicated!
She decided to be by his side forever,
If not as a lover,
But as a friend,
For love also meant sacrifice for her!

Cupid's Arrow

She wandered so long through the barren fields of loneliness,
Always hoping to one day find a love, to end her search for happiness.
So many men looked upon her beauty with empty hearts,
Piercing her wounded soul with their cold and lustful eyes.
They stripped her of her dignity,
Scanned by X-ray eyes that saw nothing at all.
She wanted to be seen as more than the object of a man's desire.
God had blessed her with such beauty, but it felt like a curse.
She was seen but not seen; no one stops to see
That inner beauty she holds inside.
Love for her seemed always out of reach,
But she knew in her heart there was love somewhere,
Someone who would look on her and truly see her for who she was,
To claim her as his Queen and sweep her off her feet.
This was her dream, though she didn't need a Prince Charming.
She was not looking for status or fame; she just wanted to feel loved.
To love and be loved in return was worth more than gold.
A pure love, a simple love, but she had lost all hope of dreams such as this.
Then out of the blue, Cupid took pity and fired a love arrow her way.
Love struck her in her heart; she felt those butterflies in her chest.
It was as if he had crossed time and space, pulled by a higher power.
She knew him instantly, though they had never met before.
Something in his eyes, his smile, made her feel like a girl again.
This just felt right, a perfect moment in time.
She blushed when he said, "Will you be my Valentine...?"

Pool of Tears

She gazed into the clear pool of loneliness.
So many shed tears had fallen into its still waters.
Then, she felt a cool breeze blow through her hair,
Ripples carried upon the once-still water.
She felt a presence as if kissed by the wind.
Then, she saw a face reflected into the pool of tears.
It was her love; even in his absence he was there.
He was with her, standing by her side, holding her hand.
She wasn't sad anymore, for she no longer felt alone.
He would soon be with her; she smiled at his reflection
And whispered, "I know..."

Those Twilight Hours

The pain of her loneliness
Hurt far more than any ailment.
She now missed him so much.
Heartache is a pain like no other.
Complaining would do her no good.
How could she describe the pain inside,
For she knew love was her only cure?
"Fate, why have you been so unkind?" she cried.
No, there was love out there somewhere, waiting!
She would cry herself to sleep at night,
But in her slumber, she would dream of him,
How he would hold her safely in his arms,
The warmth of his skin pressed against hers.
That moment when they both kissed,
She hugged her pillow and wished it was him.
This was their time, a dream sleep moment
When two hearts, two souls, connected into one.
This was why she loved to sleep,
For dreams do not stop any boundaries or oceans.
Now, she could reach out her hand, and he was there.
For now, she felt him close to her heart
As she drifted to sleep in those twilight hours.

Rise Again

Will her hopes rise again?
Her soul cries, it never lies,
Abandoned, forever lost in the moment,
Trapped in the darkness.
Even her shadow has disowned her,
Just like a rose trampled onto the floor.
She has given up hope of rising once more.
No one can see her pain or understands,
Her spirit now broken by life's constant demands.
She has given so much of her compassionate soul,
Her heart now left broken, it no longer feels whole.
She carries this burden and never complains.
Her smile long since departed, just the sadness remains.
She suffers in silence in this unfortunate state,
Longing to be touched by the kind hand of fate.
Always a fighter, she has battled the odds.
She holds out for love, for she has a deep trust in God.
No bird can fly free when it has broken its wings.
She just needs time to heal to get over such things.
There is a light at the end of the tunnel; hope is in sight.
Her confidence now growing, she heads for the light.
She basks in the sunshine, her spirit can fly.
This bird now has her wings back, she can soar in the sky.
A rose once was trampled but has come back in full bloom.
Her smile, so long absent, now lights up the room.
Sometimes, fate can be kind, and life is not as bad as it seems.
She seized her second chance to fulfill her dreams.
Like a phoenix from the ashes, this bird will fly.
The flames of her passion will light up the sky...

Missing You

I rise and check my phone,
If there was a call or text from you.
You are the first thought on my mind.
Though distant, I can feel you smile.
It's the look in your eyes
That takes my breath away,
Assuring me that you will never leave me
But love me the way I am.
Without hesitation, I rented out my heart.
It is the perfect place where love can stay.
If wishes could come true,
I would want to be with you,
Right this moment to be in your arms,
For each day that passes creates a void
That can only be filled by you, my love.
I miss you more than words can say.
Why can't I be with you? I miss you so much.
Love crosses all borders that keep us apart.
Our love will find a way to be together; I can feel it in my heart.
'Til then, the shadows of your love will keep me warm,
For I can feel your presence coursing through my veins...

Sleeping Beauty

She slept like sleeping beauty,
As if she was cast under a magical spell.
No elixir was found to cure her ills
As she slumbers alone, resigned to her fate
That never again would she feel love's gentle touch,
For she seemed to be a curse, but she never knew why,
A beautiful rose trapped in a cage surrounded by thorns.
No man dared save; she was left, lost, and alone.
Often, she dreamed of the day a hero would come,
A knight in shining armor upon a milk-white steed,
Battling his way through the storms that barred his path,
Crossing borders, fighting adversity, trying so hard to reach her side,
To kiss her sweet lips to make her his own.
She feels his kiss inside her dream; it feels so real, she opens her eyes,
Only to find herself still trapped in the dark world of her own self-doubt.
Mocking voices inside her mind keep saying her dreams never come true.
In reality, her destiny was written for her to be alone.
She was wrapped up in despair, tied down with the shackles of her mind.
Was this really how her life would be, could her future be so bleak,
Drowning in sorrow with no lifeline to hold?
But then she heard a voice cut through the darkness as if it were a knife.
It was the voice of a man calling out, "Is anyone there?"
She listened in stunned silence. Was this a trick of the mind?
She cried out to stop this madness. "Please, let me be and go away.
I have accepted my fate. Why can't you leave me alone?"
The voice louder now shouted, "I have come so far. Did I really come in vain?"
Then she realized the voice was real. The blackness cleared so she could see.
There before her stood a man she had seen in her dreams
So many nights before.
Tears rolled down her cheeks from her dark eyes.
He whispered, "Please don't cry." And he wiped away her tears.
For the first time, she felt safe and held him so tight.
He lifted her into his arms and carried her away.
She told him, "In my heart I knew that you would come."
He kissed her softly and said, "Be my queen."
She told him she would be his until life's curtain finally falls...

Bless My Soul

I wonder what life would be like without a soul?
Would I become nothing more than a robot,
Just going through life to find it had no meaning?
To find out at the last second there is nothing there?
I could not live to die that way; my soul is my light!
It guides me so I can shine forth to aid those in darkness,
To help revive their broken spirit to make them see
The beauty of this thing we call life; to make them smile!
I want to wipe away the tears from crying eyes,
To spread love and joy, instead of battling with hate and fear.
I want to live life to the fullest, to fill my heart with love,
So when on that day my heart stops beating
And my body returns to dust,
I will know my soul will live on forever...

Child...

I gave you my laughter
That you may know joy.
I gave you my peace
That you may breathe with ease.
I gave you my spirit
That you may stay strong.

You don't have a right
To end this life,
'Cause it is me you destroy when you attempt to kill your pain.

I AM not only with you...
I AM the lifeblood that courses through your veins!

I AM the light you keep in shadows.
I AM as much you,
As you are me...

No Turning Back

You left me without a second thought,
Leaving me lost in a state of darkness.
I tried to gather the remnants of my broken heart,
But the pieces no longer fit together.
I found myself looking at our wedding album.
Where was the man I married; were you always just a lie?
I wore a white dress, you wore a fake smile,
As fake as the promise to love me forever.
Instead of soft kisses on our honeymoon, I felt the sting of your hand.
I bore the pain of your punches, for I made a vow,
For better or worse, unto death do us part.
I thought you loved me, but I was wrong.
Even when we were together, your eyes were somewhere else.
The flame of passion I once felt from you now grew cold.
As you grew colder towards me, I'd cry myself to sleep.
You were still right here, only I lost you.
It was then I found myself, and I didn't want you back.
I walked away and never looked back.
There was nothing back there I wanted to see.
I cried myself to sleep, I felt so alone,
But I knew in my soul it was the right thing to do.
The love I had for you fizzled out; my love had run dry.
You moved on to another without a backward glance.
If you would only look to see what you left behind,
But time moves on, and I move with the times.
Just like time there is no turning back.
My future lies waiting ahead for me.
Now my heart is healed, I hope to find love again,
Or I hope that love finds me...

Passion

Passion for writing,
Passion for reading,
Passion for painting,
Passion for singing,
Passion for sport,
Passion for love,
Passion that steals my rest
But calms my soul!

A drive that thrives on possibilities-
Fueled by positivity!

To serve and lift the struggler-
To raise the broken ones,
To train my focus from
The one of me
To the one
Of everyone!

Passion!

Now That I've Found You

Baby I love you.
Don't leave me.
My soul has been waiting,
Yearning for your touch.
Don't leave me
Now that I've finally found you,
For you are my breaths,
My life,
And you complete me.
Like the stars complete the sky above,
You light up my darkest nights.
Without you,
I can never think of living a day.
I will feel like my own shadow has dumped me,
So stay by my side
Through thick and thin.
Promise me
You will be mine
'Til my eyes close and the grave calls me in...

Wings To Fly

She looks at the sky and thinks of him.
Her love is a distant love; she wants wings to fly,
To take to the air and land at his side,
So he can see the love that shines in her eyes.
She misses him like crazy, she wants to feel his touch,
To be held in his arms, to feel wanted and loved.
She cried herself to sleep at the sound of his voice.
When he calls her up to say goodnight,
Her heart is in pain, she feels it breaking,
Hoping one day her dreams will come true,
Wanting to be at his side to finally kiss him,
To hear his whisper, "I love you."
But now she waits, as she waits always,
Just to hear his voice when he calls to say hello.
A simple text message raises her spirit.
It gives her hope for tomorrow and brightens her day.
There is a love that crossed over boundaries;
A fantasy moment star-crossed lovers both share.
She wants to wake up and be beside him,
To feel his kiss as he touches her hair.
But she wakes up alone and to reality.
It is still only a dream, as he is not there.
If only she had wings, then off she would fly...

Chocolate Kisses

When I think of you, I need to write
Romantic lines about how I feel,
For I get lost in the moment and reminisce
Over all the times that I spent with you,
Walking hand in hand and barefoot on the beach,
Feeling the warm sand between my toes.
You chased me along the breakwater, splashing me with love.
My senses were awakened in the moments spent with you.
You pulled me close, then kissed my lips.
They tasted so sweet like a Hershey's chocolate bar.
It only made me want you more.
I felt so safe when you held me in your arms.
You made me blush like a teenage girl,
Lost in the love of a chocolate kiss...

Painted With Love

He believes in her, and she trusts him enough to let him paint her.
She becomes his perfect mural.
He captures her essence in every brush stroke,
Her life now a blank canvas,
A new beginning
As he paints her anew.
She so often felt her soul was dying,
But now she felt her emotions come to life.
What once felt dead to her was reborn
As new feelings stirred inside her.
He somehow had awakened her soul.
He could see her for what she was,
Like she was looking into a mirror for the first time.
She saw herself in his painting.
He had gifted her a perfect treasure.
His love had made her smile again,
Such a beautiful smile that had somehow been lost to her for so many years.
He sat there smiling as he painted her.
He could have stared at her forever,
For she had a certain kind of beauty hidden behind an angelic glow.
He had found his muse in her.
She was his inspiration,
Now he needed to paint.
They had found each other and touched one another's hearts;
They were soulmates...

Shepherd Of My Soul

As she lay upon her deathbed, silently weeping,
Reminiscing of past memories — the good, the bad.
Now feeling so weak, drifting to unconsciousness,
She has a vision; a radiance appears before her eyes.
It was of a book, her book — a book of life.
This was her life story opening up before her eyes.
It told of her trials and tribulations;
The hurdles she had crossed, big and small.
Then, the vision changes to footprints in the sand.
A disfigured man now walked beside her.
He held her hand and gently smiled.
She could see he was bleeding from head to toe,
Yet he did not complain; instead, he comforted her.
He was there for her, and she knew who he was.
How many times had she complained, "Where are you?"
During the hard times, those troubled storms of her life.
She asked him, "How long do I have to suffer?
How long will I carry the burden of such pain?
Have I not been through so many trials already?
When will I find a little happiness,
To rejoice in life, and to smile again?"
Questioning, questions yet still unanswered,
But she was answered, for now she knew.
The Good Shepherd had never left her side.
He had always walked by her side.
She felt ashamed of her trials and tribulations.
Her hardships were not easy to face,
But he had to face crucifixion for us all.
An innocent man carried the sins of the world on his shoulders;
From womb to tomb, he carried this burden alone.

From carpenter to King of the Jews,
His flesh torn out from the surge of the whip,
Taunted and beaten, battered and abused,
Denied and betrayed by the people that he loved,
Then nailed to a cross to die for our sins.
He did not waver or complain.
When he did speak to God, our Father,
It was to ask Him to forgive us.
His suffering shames me, for I complain of pain.
I know not of what true pain is,
Nor am I fit to wash his feet.
He suffers for me, for us all.
His spirit gives me strength to endure.
I feel his power inside me as he holds my hand.
Who am I to complain when He is with me?
He is my path to salvation; in His footsteps I follow,
In sickness and in health,
For I have found favor in His eyes...

A Poet's Prayer

She adds color to everyone's life with her words
As she wonders to herself,
Will anyone miss her if she was gone?
Will she live on in hearts with loving memories,
Or will she be washed away like words written on a tidal beach?
She feels like a tree that has no roots.
To truly survive, she needs to spread her love.
This is a motto she has carved into her heart,
But how long can her heart beat on?
As she starts to think, all hope is gone,
But a hope still flickers in a tiny flame.
In need of a miracle, she prays to the divine,
Hoping her prayers are answered and given more time
To realize her dreams, to get a second chance,
To write more chapters in her book of life,
To become someone's queen, to be a bride,
The chance to find love with another,
To be blessed to become a mother,
To be loved as she loves.
As she kneels and prays to God above.
To herself she gently weeps
Before she peacefully falls to sleep...

A Mother's Love

She saw a bright light in the sky.
It seemed to be calling out to her,
"Come to me," and she wanted to go
To find peace and solace
Until she heard another voice,
Telling her, beseeching her to wait.
"My child, I love you,
I need you;
Don't add to my heartache.
Stay with me or take me with you.
I have lost one child, I cannot lose you.
You are my life, you bring me hope."
She listened to the voice as she looked to the sky.
Making her choice, she chose to stay.
For the sake of her mother's love,
She could not bear to give her mother more heartbreak...

Love Loosed

What would I have done
If I hadn't met you?

I would have lived a life
In broken pieces,
Molten with pain,
Withered like an autumn flower.

Your love scooped up the broken shards of me,
Sculpting me anew,
Bound with a love I'd never known.

Clearing the weeds,
You planted your seed
That I might know my bloom!

I felt I had butterfly wings
As you added endless colors to the blank velvet canvas of me...
Exposing new shades of life
And setting me to flight.

All the love that was stored in me
Began to breathe as you unearthed my buried soul,
Lifting me by the heart and massaging it to life.

It wasn't easy to trust.
It wouldn't be easy to love.
You knew our love would be tested
And weather many storms,
But you knew we could...
Knew we would.

How long could I stay away?
How long would I be ignorant to your love?
My soul wasn't mine any longer.
We are now twice the blossom together!

The Love Regained

He didn't feel she was a mere colleague.
The sparks between them had burned brightly,
Even she couldn't deny that.
They had spent days together
That had been more intriguing
Than the merger they were both supposed to be working on.
She was beautiful and loving,
But she felt she wouldn't ever fit in any man's life
Because of the scars the past had imprinted on her memory screen.
And she preferred to go unnoticed,
Even in a crowd,
She so cleverly concealed from everyone.
His eyes followed her
Wherever she went.
He sensed the pain,
The pain she silently endured.
He knew there was more to her,
Though she appeared mysterious,
And he wanted to hug her
But was afraid of losing her,
For he knew she couldn't be his,
As she was already taken, someone else's.
Then, they drifted apart
As she no longer worked with him,
But what's destined can't be avoided,
For he bumped into her several years later,
And now her relationship status had changed.

The flame in him had never died
As she frequently haunted his thoughts,
And now he needed her to be by his side
And couldn't let fate win in keeping her away.
He approached her reluctantly
And asked her to be a part of his life,
Was afraid she would decline his proposal
And prayed in his heart
That she would accept him.
After much thinking,
She wondered how this can be true?
How can love knock once more
At her heart's door?
She found the love she'd always wanted in him;
A caring, compassionate partner
Who made her feel like she's on Cloud Nine,
And life suddenly opened a new chapter for them
Where love passed the test of time
And finally survived...

Streams of Consciousness

As she sat looking in front of the mirror,
She could see the reflection of a teenage girl smiling back.
A sudden pain stung her soul as memories came flooding back.
Scars from the past opened, once more tearing her heart apart.
She realized her life had changed so much, and it was not for the better.
Slowly, she began to turn back the pages of time in her book of life.
It was as if she could see a scrapbook of images in her mind's eye.
Memories of when she turned sweet sixteen flashed into her head.
From a pretty bud she had now blossomed into a beautiful rose.
She was so pleasing to the eye it was as if she was meant to be seen.
People praised her beauty, yet she doubted herself.
The road ahead for her seemed sunny and bright
As the door of opportunities opened to the world before her,
But she shunned the bright city lights and chose nature, instead.
She preferred a simple contentment found in the littlest of things;
The fresh scent of flowers carried on a summer's breeze,
To dance like a child in the first falling monsoon rains,
Soaked to the skin as if she had been baptized.
She saw a world of wonder through her dark brown eyes.
Life was for living, and she lived hers to the fullest.
Daring to be herself, she was gentle and kind,
Though she would often dream as young girls do
Of falling in love with a handsome Prince;
To find the right man and fall in love.
She dreamed of walking hand in hand, of that first kiss.

Where would he take her on their first date?
She would lie in bed awake, and yet she dreamed,
Lost in her thoughts of finding true love.
She wanted to be taken, to be wanted and loved.
Was this too much to ask, for it was such a simple dream?
Dreams are only dreams, and they seldom come true,
As she would discover as she journeyed through her later life,
Stuck in a loveless marriage and now a battered wife.
The pages of her life were now full of sorrow,
But she still lived in the hope of a brighter tomorrow.
Those pages of her past were marked with pain.
She would never go back to that kind of man again,
But she had learnt so many lessons from her book of life.
She had found the way forward, no longer the child.
As she looked upon the young girl in the mirror, she waved goodbye.
It was her time to be a woman, to be the rose...

Lourdes Alexander

The Treasure

She painted the sunsets
In different shades with her smile.
She showed him love was indeed worthwhile,
For he believed love never existed
As he had never ever really tasted.
She mystically brought him
Into her beautiful world;
A world that she had created herself...
There, she showed him
Her true self;
A different she
When she was with him.
She had reserved the best parts of her
Only for him,
For many knew—
She had a heart of gold,
But she opened doors
That she had once closed,
Only to him.
She wanted him to realize
She was the one - His Eve
That would complete
And fill his paradise.
He saw through her beautiful soul,
Realized she was the once-in-a-lifetime kind of love
Whom his soul sought for
And wanted to grow old.
It was neither lust
Nor desire for her, he knew.
He had in fact tasted her spirituality
That cleansed like fire,
Out of the blue,
And it was so pure and so true...
So, he couldn't imagine a life without her.
He needed her to be his,
As she was undefinable!

Thinking Of You

I'm lost in my thoughts,
Be it night or day,
Wondering how life would be
With you by my side,
Hugging and cuddling you,
Kissing and making love with you.
I wonder, am I the first one
You think of as you rise?
Am I your last thought
As you drift to sleep?
Do I cross your mind
While you're at work?
Or do you remember me
Only when you receive
A text from me,
For I can't stop thinking of you
As my life revolves around you.
I smile,
I cry,
I blush,
I miss,
As your name is always now
On my lips...

The Heart of Loving

(Collaboration by Lourdes Alexander and Philip Matogo)

(Lourdes)

What a woman
Needs from a man
Is not too hard to define.
Every woman
Wants a man
Who handles her with care,
Who clasps his arms around her,
Watches her sleep,
Strokes her hair,
Never lets her forget that
She's beautiful,
Drowns in her eyes,
Reads her thoughts,
Loves her tenderly,
Reminds her,
"You're mine, Baby."

Makes her feel
She is the one for whom
His life was created,
Allows her to spread her wings and fly,
Calls her his Goddess, his Queen,
Treats her as his equal
With dignity and respect,
Stands by her side,
Encourages her when she is down,
Is faithful even when she is not around,
Gets on his knees
To profess his love
By confessing
He wants to be her man.
Is there such a gentleman?
She wonders,
For when she finds him
She'd never let him go,
Would be his
'Til her life ends.
He,
Her new chapter,
The reason she smiles...
She'd then reserve
Her days,
Her nights,
Her time,
Every hour,
Every minute,
Every second
For her man.

(Philip)

A man falls in love but twice.
In my case, that would be thrice.
With a woman who's her, herself and us,
No need for much ado frills or fuss.
A man seeks the Holy Trinity in a woman,
For in the eyes of a woman, he sees God in a woman.
It's not in her smile or liquid grace
Or the perfection of her face.
It's in eyes windowing her soul
So he can look into himself and become whole.
Love is a word that cannot be put into words, yes.
I want more from a woman than to get her out of her dress,
For hot passion shall evanesce,
And the suppleness of a woman's bust
Is just a prelude to the ultimate dust;
As we shall all die and be cast unto sullen winds, yes.
Beneath azure skies, decaying leaves are shed, no less,
But a man's love for a woman is endless,
Even when it starts as more and ends less.
If you want me to kneel, I shall rise,
For when I kneel, I rise in your eyes.
I shall not call you a queen.
Such fulsome praise is too lean.
You are a goddess with a small G.
A big one would make you more than just for me,
And I don't want to share you with anyone.
When a man loves a woman, she's the only One.

99% Angel

Staring at her with a smile,
His brain seemed to explode
As he scrutinized her red gown,
Scanning what she wore beneath,
Stripping her bare
And seeing through her femininity,
Pawing her,
Devouring her,
Penetrating her,
Owning her.
She could read his wild thoughts,
For she knew him well enough.
She was almost an angel in her entirety.
But there was that 1% devil in her too,
Which she would never let anyone have a peekaboo.
She hid the secrets of her desire,
Though her passion burned in her like fire;
Her wild thoughts,
Where she too stripped him naked
In her mind's eyes
And made love with him,
Though she always hid from him,
Her unsatiated passion
Burying her pent-up emotions,
Cause that's how she loved to stay.
She preferred love over lust,
For she believed love was pure and divine
And wouldn't compromise on her values for lust
But would be subservient to her man
When the time is right.
So, she preferred to live like an innocent child
Until that day he would take her as his bride...

As She Flutters By...

She felt warm and secure, curled up in her favorite blanket,
Though life has a way of shaking you awake.
It woke her out of her silken cocoon,
Transforming her into a butterfly overnight,
Forcing her to face up to the hardships of life,
As she looked back over past memories
That still hung in her mind like a distant dream.
She wanted to go back there, but she knew she never could.
Many now praised her external beauty.
Men wanted to hold her, to win her heart,
As she now fluttered from one flower bud to another,
Forever searching for her one true companion;
One who could still see the caterpillar in her too,
Loving her innocence,
Who would laugh at her silly jokes,
To accept her for who she truly was.
She knew he was out there waiting for her somewhere,
So she fluttered on the wing in search of love,
Hoping for her loneliness to come to an end...

Thinking Of You (Part 2)

The moment she read his old message,
Memories flashed back;
The love they once had,
The way he once made her glad,
Couldn't stand her feeling sad,
But things changed and things turned bad.
She remembered vividly
The time when she used to wait
To just receive a text or two from him,
The time when she used to wait
To hear his voice and see him,
But then he left,
Creating a wound,
Giving her a scar
That she didn't want to forget,
For though the scar was painful,
She wished that he'd one day return and say
I'm here, my love,
I had never gone far away...
So, she took her phone and then began to type a text...

"Hey,

I was scrolling through our previous conversations. Never has a day gone by
when I have never missed you nor erased you from my thoughts. I have
been waiting anxiously to hear from you. My soul has been waiting to
connect with yours.

I would like to make an honest confession, for I realized that my words were not enough for you. They couldn't bring you back, for I had often relentlessly tried. Nor could my tears melt your heart because I had often silently cried. You left me like a rose trampled in the cold. Frozen.

I survived cherishing good old memories, but I never wanted only happy memories. All I ever longed for was you.

So, I hope this confession of mine finds you in the mood to re-bloom this feeling yet once again, because I'm sure you too have been missing from love for far too long.

Thinking of you.

I always will..."

A Voice In The Darkness

Sadness, it gripped her.
Loneliness stung her.
The darkness, it scared her.
Her shadow disowned her.
Grasping at straws, out of her depth,
Drowning in her sleep,
Gasping for breath,
She couldn't breathe as the dark night closed in.
The air felt so cold, caressing her skin.
She tried to scream out, but her voice got choked.
It felt like invisible fingers gripping her throat.
She had entered the lost world, the labyrinth of death,
Her heartbeat so fast, but it was stealing her breath.
Trapped on all sides by the darkness, she started falling.
From out of nowhere, she heard a voice faintly calling,
"Please don't leave like this, we love you so much!"
Out of the darkness, she felt her mother's loving touch.
"Your story isn't over yet; there is so much to live for,
New chapters to be written, new things to explore.
I taught you to fight, I taught you to win.
Fight now for life, child, don't you dare give in."
Her mother's voice guided her back out of the dream.
She fought through the darkness and let out a scream.
Waking up dazed, she was lost and surprised,
But the first thing she saw was her mother's loving eyes.
Her mother held her so tightly, both of them cried.
"My child, I love you so much I thought you had died."
Nothing in this life is quite what it seems.
Was this a near death experience or just a bad dream...?

Second Chance

He wanted her to reach for the stars,
To rediscover her inner self, her missing smile.
Life, it was for living in the pursuit of love.
She had been cut off from her feelings for far too long.

All she wanted was to trust again,
To find the one true love, to share her soul.
Her heart's desires were for simple things;
A gentle touch from a loving hand.

He was life's gift to her — a second chance.
She needed nothing but to feel loved,
Held tight and warm in his safe embrace.
She longed for him, to be held in his arms.

He was her lifeline that would save her from herself,
To pull her free from her ocean of self-doubt.
The only waves she felt now were her emotions for him.
If she had to drown, then it would be in his eyes...

Revived In Love

He left her without any reason,
Making her drown in misery.
She didn't have any clue of time or season
As she walked in darkness and despair.
Her shadow seemed to have ditched her too.
The forbidden fruit — love;
Why, when she had tasted, had she felt
Love was like venom?
Stung her soul,
Pierced her heart,
Locked her down.
She lived but felt lifeless.
That's when he walked into her life,
Giving her the will to survive.
She bloomed again from a withered flower
As he filled her soul with love.
Reluctantly, she opened,
All the pains seemed to have instantly vanished.
She didn't know the forbidden fruit — love
Would really fascinate her yet once again.

Radiance shone on her face.
The minute his eyes met hers,
She too rescued his soul
By bringing out the best in him.
A selfless love she bestowed.
He would do anything to be with her,
As she filled his empty space!
He painted different shades in her life,
Adorning her with beauty.
He took her into another realm,
His beautiful world
Where they both
Loved,
Laughed,
Lived,
As they found real love
In each other's arms,
To be swept away in a different world
Of existence!

Free Bird

She felt trapped inside her life.
He told her to spread her wings and fly.
"Don't be afraid of the unknown,
For no one knows the future.
Come fly to me upon the winds of change.
I will be here to catch you if you fall.
Let me be your pillow.
I will keep you safe from harm.
Fly to me, free bird, fly to me..."

Love Crossed Path

Suddenly, I felt love touch me
When our lives crossed paths.
I was full of self-doubt and suspicion,
Thinking a love such as this can't last.
I tried to hide my true feelings by playing silly games,
But he saw through my disguise, and my love for him remained.
Days and weeks sometimes passed without a word being said,
Though thoughts of him, they never left my head.
He always accepted me without hesitation,
Like we were meant to be together.
I think I have found myself a soul mate, my perfect lover.
He painted a different picture of life where I felt complete.
We seemed to just connect together, with no need to compete.
The dark shadows of my past, they began to fade away.
He brought a rainbow into my life when once it looked so grey.
When the realization hit me that I loved him, I started to pray
That he would love me forever, each and every day.
I feel so blessed, I want our love to last.
Now, I look toward the future, instead of living in the past...

Into The Mist

(Collaboration by Marina Malhotra and Lourdes Alexander)

(Marina Malhotra)

There is a fog in the distance
As the mist slowly rolls in.
A bell tolls out, breaking the silence.
Like a white blanket, it covers the earth.
Almost a dream, I feel lost in its touch.
I hear a voice softly calling my name.
Lost in the fog, a light forth does shine.
From out of the ether, I see her appear.
Flowers spring up where she has walked.
Butterflies flutter round her head in a crown made of wings.
The bell now falls silent as birds start to sing.
Leaves fall at her feet to carpet the ground.
As she banishes the shadows, the sun now appears.
She welcomes the sun with her beautiful smile.
As the fog falls to the floor, it cries at her feet.
Spiderwebs shine for her, full of wet morning dew.
As the sun now rises, as if just for her.
The blue sky and the ocean shine in her eyes,
Reflecting the beauty that she has in her heart...

(Lourdes Alexander)

As she walks slowly through the early morning mist,
Cautiously she treads softly, minding each step.
Try to go unnoticed, leaving no footprints upon the lawn,
She wants to find solitude to be alone,
To escape into the mist to get lost in her thoughts,
So often chastised and judged for her looks.
Men only saw her beauty, but she was so much more,
Tired of unwanted attention of so many prying eyes.
The mist was a blanket to shroud her in its gentle embrace.
She always felt in sync with nature, like it was her friend.
Mother Nature knew her as a true free-spirited soul.
She walks into the mist, and for the first time she smiles.
The sadness on her face now fades and drifts away.
As a warm breeze touches her cheek, it feels like a kiss of pure love.
Her golden hair glows as the sun starts to shine down.
The birds all start singing as the butterflies flutter by.
A cool breeze envelopes and drifts through the trees.
The rustling leaves seem to whisper her name
As the shadows come out and dance at her feet.
Even alone in the mist, her presence is known.
She still gets noticed wherever she goes...

Whisper Softly

Whisper to me sweet words of nothingness.
Let your breath do the talking.
Take me with you to a different plane of existence
Where there's just you and me,
Where the sky is our roof,
Where the earth is our home,
Where I lay beside you,
Holding you close to me.
We only have eyes for each other.
Will you find such a place?
Will you be happy to be with me?
Am I enough for you?
Or would you need someone?
I don't have to worry
If my hair is all messed up.
I don't have to worry
If I look good naturally,
For I would find it
As your eyes and lips
Will do the talking...

Angels Amongst Us

The children were all sitting quietly in their class
When the teacher asked, "Do you believe in angels?"
All the children put their hands in the air and shouted, "Yes!"
"Has anyone seen an angel?" the teacher inquired.
She got no response to this; the class went silent,
When out from the back of the class a voice said, "Yes."
All the children laughed out loud and jeered,
For at the back of the room on his own sat little Johnny.
He was often on his own, seen as a slow learner,
A quiet boy often untidy with unkempt hair and dirty clothes.
The teacher walked over to him and thought Johnny was being foolish.
"So tell us, Johnny, where did you happen to see this angel of yours?"
All the children laughed again, and Johnny blushed with shame,
But then he stood up and began to speak; the laughter stopped.
He said, "Teacher, I see my mother as an angel who loves and protects me.
She makes sacrifices every day to make my life a little better.
Sometimes when I wet the bed, she lifts me to where it is dry.
She sleeps where it is wet, and she never complains.
I fall asleep safe in her arms; she never gets angry but keeps me warm.
My father is an angel.
He works so hard to put food on the table and clothes on my back.
He works long hours and is always tired, but he reads me stories
When I can't sleep.

I see a little angel when my baby sister cries.
She is so innocent of everything.
Angels walk amongst us every day, only people don't see them
For the good they do.
I see angels now here in this class too;
My friends who help me when I struggle with my work,
Friends who I play with who make me laugh, each one spreads a little joy.
Finally, Teacher, I see an angel in you for the patience you show me
Because I'm slow.
You are always kind and try to help me; that is what angels do."
The teacher looked on at little Johnny; she couldn't speak
As tears started rolling down her cheek.
This little boy who most deemed slow
Had given her the greatest compliment anyone could ever give.
She looked on at Johnny; she felt ashamed.
She knew then that this boy was no fool.
Sometimes we just need the chance to speak out and truly shine.
When Johnny sat down, all his classmates stood up.
Everybody clapped and gave him a big round of applause
Because they knew what he said was true.
Angels walk amongst us, and they are everywhere...

To Be A Butterfly...

As she walked through her garden, she reminisced,
Remembering all the moments she had spent with him.
She wanted to be with him, again at his side.
Smiling at her memories, she softly began to cry.
Just at that very moment, two butterflies appeared,
Such beautiful creatures and so carefree.
As they fluttered by her and from one flower to another,
This made her think even more of her distant lover.
She thought how marvelous it would be to have butterfly wings,
To fly freely with her lover to do such things.
All she would have to do is flap her wings and she would fly
On the wind to her lover and be at his side.
One of the butterflies seemed to understand
As it flew over to her and landed on her hand.
The butterfly whispered, "Close your eyes and see.
If you believe in miracles, then come now, fly with me."
She felt wing sprout from her back, and she fluttered on the breeze.
As she took to the sky with a gentle grace and ease,
The butterfly told her, "Your lover is waiting, he misses you;
Miracles can happen when a love is true."
She kept her eyes tightly closed as she flew high into the air.
Time lost all meaning, and in seconds she was there.
She landed beside her lover and fell into his arms.
Both got lost in the moment of magic and charm.
When she opened her eyes, the butterfly was gone,
But the taste of her lover's lips, it lingered on.
The words of the butterfly fluttered in her head.
She woke up hugging her pillow, alone in her bed.
Her lover was gone, they never said goodbye.
Oh, how she wished she could be a butterfly...

Never Forget Her Name...

She was but a child, still a bud not yet a flower,
A pretty smile, joyful in her own little world.
Yet for one so young, she was denied the chance to blossom,
For this little girl was deflowered by cruel lustful men,
As strangled by common weeds, they stole her little life away.
She was too trusting of evil men, innocent of such ways.
To be stolen like her innocence, she was abducted off the street.
A day that started off with the promise of such joy would end
With the promise of death.
She had no idea what the future had in store, how could she?
Dreams of dance class, of ice-cream sundaes;
These were things she probably thought,
Only to find herself facing the worst kind of monsters.
Each of these monsters had lust in their eyes and cold, empty hearts.
They stole her innocence as she cried for mercy, again and again,
Used and abused.
Her once pretty smile now lost forever; her petals all broken fall to the floor.
She has seen horrors no one should witness;
She has felt pain that no one should feel,
But these men know she has seen their faces,
So to hide their shame and cover their guilt,
They kill this beautiful child, this sweet little rosebud as she lies helpless.
No mercy is shown as they take her young life, trying to protect their own.
Monsters are real, they walk amongst us; what makes them scary,
They look just like us.
An innocent child, trusting of adults, fell victim to the monsters
And the things that they do.
Her tiny body lies broken and discarded, but we must remember her name,
For her soul cries for justice
Now pressed at God's bosom.
She looks up and asks Him...
"Lord, what did I do wrong to be punished with such a horrible fate?"
For she has no voice now; it was cruelly stolen, so we must speak up for her
So her tiny soul can at least lie in peace. We are her voice,
The voice of a nation
Who can shout out, "We will not let this happen, no never again..."

Waiting For Love

She waited in the airport lounge, waiting for her flight to be called.
Her heart felt heavy for a love she had to leave behind,
Hoping with all hope that he would come for her.
She hoped he would drop down at her feet and beg her not to go,
To tell her that he loved her and couldn't survive without her,
That she was the very air he breathed, and her love was like oxygen.
She scanned the room for passengers, but each was just a stranger.
The face she wanted to see before her, it sadly wasn't there.
Over the airport tannoy, her place was set for boarding.
Picking up her luggage, she wept because she knew it was time to go.
Walking to the checkout desk, ticket in hand and crying,
She knew this was the end of love and another broken heart.
Her head told her to forget him, but her heart wouldn't let her.
But she knew on this life's journey, she would travel on alone.
But at that moment, she heard it, her name was being called out.
Over the loud speaker she heard the words,
"I love you, Baby, won't you stay?"
Her heart, it did a somersault and when she turned, she saw him.
She dropped her luggage to the floor and ran into his arms.
He told her that he loved her and to never leave him.
Wherever they would travel, they would never be alone...

Child Of The Night

While the world sleeps peacefully in their beds,
She walks the dimly lit streets on her own,
Trying to catch the eyes of a new customer walking by.
Her pride long since swallowed, now out turning tricks,
Fresh meat for the one, offered to the wolf with hungry eyes.
She dresses like a woman, but she is just a frightened child,
Selling herself for money to dirty men with filthy minds.
Her dreams long since lost, only her nightmares come true.
This little beautiful butterfly often gets beaten black and blue.
She is but a ghost of a child, she is past caring anymore.
Her tears long since run dry, her little body wracked in pain,
But tomorrow she will be forced back on the streets again...

Seeing Each Other

He woke up from a sleep that was not a sleep,
His mind did not feel like his own,
His recollections were hazy, his memory unsure.
He could see a silhouette, a shape of a woman sitting beside him,
Like a negative image of a photograph before its development stage.
Something about her made him feel that he knew her.
As his eyes started to clear, he could now see her face.
Was she his wife, a friend, or a lover?
He didn't know, he just couldn't recall.
She could read by his face, he was in a state of confusion.
Smiling, she assured him everything would be fine.
He took comfort in her gentle reassurance.
She seemed so familiar, but he didn't know why.
The doctors told him he had been in a bad accident.
He had been in a coma and damaged his brain.
She held his hand tightly, smiling yet weeping.
His memory had been taken as if by a thief in the night.
She didn't rush him or bombard him with old memories.
He would discover their love, but it would take time.
She had a secret, but she couldn't tell him
Her eyesight was failing; she was going blind,
But as their love blossomed, he knew that he loved her,
So she told him her secret, and he broke down and cried.
He said he would love her and protect her forever.
"Love," he whispered, "is said to be blind."
She shed a tear, and he gently wiped it.
That's when he kissed her and said,
"You don't need to see me to know that I'm here..."

Dream Sleep

Sleep should have been her sweet release,
But she would carry her troubles into her dreams.
She had made her bed, and she slept on it.
As she slept, her subconscious drifted.
It pulled her into the darkest of dreams,
Choking her, so she gasped for breath,
Strangled by the dark hands of the night.
A darkness seemed to settle upon her soul.
As the shadows taunted her, cruelly they mocked.
She stirred in her sleep, trying to wake,
But the shadows, they held her, pulling her down.
The candle of hope was her flickering flame.
When it finally burnt out, she knew she was lost.
She felt she was falling in a well of despair,
Tumbling further into the void.
She cried out for salvation, to God to be saved.
In her moment of doubt, a light started to shine.
Far in the distance, it started to come near.
She reached for the light, and there she found God's hand.
He pulled her out of the darkness and into the light.
The shadows that held her slipped into the dark.
Those dark thoughts she had now faded to grey.
She called out to God, and He answered her prayers.
When she rose in the morning, the sun smiled on her.
The demons had been cast from out of her mind...

Answer The Door To Love

Just knocking on the door to your heart
To deliver a message, to check that you are fine.
It's just a little love poem and a reminder
That I still want you to be mine.
You know I think about you all the time.
The thought of you sends tingles down my spine.
I want to whisper into your ear that I love you
And that I wish to give you my heart.
But for now, it is just a love letter because we're far apart...

Come Dance With Me...

You took me by surprise
When you caught me off-guard
And asked me to dance.
As the DJ played your favorite romantic tune,
You led me to the middle of the spacious room,
Cajoling me to shred all nervousness
And to place my trust in you,
Spinning me gently in your arms
While placing your hands gently on my delicate waist.
As the music sped up,
We both began to sway gracefully.
Our steps didn't miss a beat
As we were in perfect sync.
And then, you pulled me closer to your body,
Into a perfect embrace as the music stopped...
When I gazed into your hazel eyes,
I couldn't help but reminisce each loving embrace
In the past
As you fed my soul
With your mysterious masculine scent,
For I breathed it, again and again,
Giving me an impression
We need to run away that split second
And make love in the woods,
Losing ourselves in a different plane of existence.
I got lost in this eternal trance.
You brought me back
When you snapped at me and asked me,
"Baby, can we stop dancing
And head straight home...?"
Seemed like you read my wild thoughts,
And you too couldn't wait any longer
To be entwined like branches
While our bodies sleep, cradled together
In the depths of love
Like one heart forever...

Come the Rain

She sits stark by the window pane,
Watching the droplets of rain.
The aroma of freshly brewed coffee filled the air,
Eliciting her buried desire,
Racing her heart
In flames,
In fire.
Sweet memories of making out
That she had beautifully etched in her heart,
Lingered in her mind
Even in his absence.
She felt his touch coursing through her veins,
Lost in thoughts of him.
She didn't realize he walked into the room.
He hugged her tightly.
His touch ignited fire on her skin,
And she shivered at the sensation.
He ran his hands through her unkempt but shiny locks,
Signaling to her what's gonna follow.
She was subservient to his manly desire;
Together they melted in passion...

My Craziness

Love made me a dreamer,
Lost in your thoughts,
Missing you like crazy
Every second when you aren't around.
I feel distant and lonely,
Checking and reading your old texts,
Over and over again
So that I feel your presence,
But the sadness doesn't seem to vanish.
I don't feel like talking to anyone;
Become tongue-tied and absolutely silent.
Tears flow without reason.
A grief strikes me.
Don't understand
What's happening to me.
Should I go away from you?
Far, far away?
Will then I be able to be myself once again?
I know it's impossible,
For how can I breathe without you, my air?
How can I?

A Divine Perception

Your eyes secretly speak to me,
The feelings you so easily suppress.
There's so much you have to say,
But you can't express and hold onto it.
I see fear in them,
The shadows of your past,
Chasing and taunting you.
I see you laughing,
But your soul is crying from within, through them.
Tell me, my love,
What hurts you?
What have you treasured in your heart?
For so long, I've been your shadow.
You don't need to hide anything,
For nothing else matters to me
Than your smile...
Let's enjoy this journey together,
Wiping each other's tears away.
I am ready in all ways.
Can you trust in me
Without any inhibitions or fears?
I pledge to fill up the void with my love.
Hopefully, that's what you need,
For nothing else really matters.
Your heart is quite safe
With mine....

A Once Frozen Heart

Your love has melted my frozen heart.
I feel the warmth of love in my icy veins;
A feeling I never thought I would sense again.
As my heart beats once more, I breathe in your love.
I feel we are waves, waves of emotions,
Together forever, never to part.
I once felt so empty, but that feeling has gone,
Replaced now with joy as your love fills my heart.
When I think of you, my cheeks start to blush,
Warmed by my blood that pumps so fast for you.
I once felt so sad, but now I am aglow.
People, they notice that I now wear a smile.
Unknowingly, I've changed, and it's because I found love in you.
I so want to kiss you and hold you so tight.
You are the reason why things feel so right.
I think of you with me;
I will dream of you tonight...

Living the Nightmare

I thought I had paved myself a new road.
Life was beautiful; I had a new direction.
I was heading to new pastures; I felt carefree again.
But it didn't last; the dark shadows of my past follow me.
I can't seem to shake them, they haunt my sleep.
They creep into my bed at night and get into my head.
Why can't they leave me? Is a little peace too much to ask?
I once was happy and carefree, but it feels like a lifetime ago.
These shadows that haunt me, I thought had finally died,
A corpse to be burned in the ashes and scattered on the winds of change.
But I was wrong; I was so wrong, why did they return?
They came back disguised as friends hiding behind a masked smile.
I surrendered myself blindly to them, like a trusting fool.
The shadows crawled over me once more, and I cannot break free.
It feels like I am being swallowed up in a pit of despair.
Is this it, is this going to be my end...?
Will I ever get the chance to start afresh,
To be me, to be the me I know I can be?
But I feel so trampled and crushed, a prisoner of my past.
Will I succumb and give in? Will the shadows drag me down?
I can't sleep; the night terrors wake me from my slumber.
Silently, I scream, my heart racing; I am covered in sweat.
It is like I have seen a ghost, and the ghost is me.
This dream, this nightmare, will not go away.
I feel my end is near; I live in fear every second, every second...

Living The Illusion

She couldn't shake him out of her mind,
Even though she had been cast aside by him.
Deep down, the longing to be reunited still burned deep inside her heart.
She saw him in her dreams.
She thought of him when she woke.
It was as if time stood still, but the days moved forward.
She tried to piece her life back together by living on memories,
Remembering the good times that they had shared,
The fun times, the love and laughter.
As the breeze gently touched her face,
She smiled as if she was caressed again by him,
But this touch only awoke her from her dream
That she was only living the illusion of love.
There was no point in living the lie.
She had to learn to be true to herself and to others,
So she let go of the past, those happy sad memories.
That's when she found some peace of mind...

The Music Of Love

The sound of a haunting violin melody fell upon her ears.
She wondered who was playing such a beautiful tune, her curiosity arose.
As the music drifted on the breeze, she followed the haunting tune.
She wasn't afraid; even when it led her into the forest, she walked on.
As if she was enchanted by the harmony, the chords pulled ever on.
There in a clearing, by a pond, he sat under the moonlight,
Playing the violin.
The water on the pond seemed to ripple,
Like sound waves, they danced to his tune.
He didn't realize he was being watched
Ss he closed his eyes to all but the music.
His love of music was deeper than anything, and he played so well.
She too was now lost in the music as the violin pulled at her heartstrings.
Under the full moon, she began to dance;
A dance of love, she danced for the night.
That's when he saw her as she danced in circles upon the soft grass.
He stopped playing and watched her,
But the sound of silence broke her from her trance.
She opened her eyes only to meet his; he smiled at her and she blushed.
He stepped forward.
She apologized for interrupting his beautiful tune.
"There is no need to apologize; I play this tune each night to the moon,
And you fell from the stars; will you dance for me?"
She smiled, "Yes, if you play a melody just for me."
When he played, they both got lost in the sweet music.
She danced closer and closer to him and smiled.
He stood up and took her in his arms and kissed her.
This was not love at first sight but love at first sound.
Sometimes, love can happen in the strangest of ways.
It can just call to you in the night, carried on the breeze...

The Bridge Across Time

(Collaboration by Lourdes Alexander and Lawrence Parent)

We don't know when,
We don't know how,
We don't know why
Our souls connected.

Were we supposed to be together?
Was it the pain that drew us closer?
Did the Heavens plan,
Or was it mere coincidence?

We can't ignore the feeling.
We can't hold on now.
We yearn to be with each other
Every passing day.

Can love be complicated?
Wasn't love supposed to be just loved?
Should we stop
Or just listen to our hearts and go on?

There's no need to be sorry.
There's no need to ignore.
'Cause it's not desire of the flesh
But pure love, care, and concern we have for each other.

Let's forget what the world would say.
Let's forget the speculating eyes.
They weren't there to heal our wounds,
But it was love which mended our brokenness.

Our love gave us a will to survive,
Bringing peace into our broken lives.
Let's live this moment,
For it was not by chance we met, but we were destined to be together.

Everything touches,
Everything spans the chasm between us.
Now is our need,
Holding hands for eternity.
We sigh,
Our breath traveling across,
Into each other,
Divine.

Soul of time,
Heart of need,
Meet me there...

The Phoenix In Her Heart

She withered like a fallen leaf on an autumn wind,
Yet she was barely out of the summer of her years.
Hopes of survival seemed a distant dream.
She had to pick herself emotionally up off the ground.
Like the fabled phoenix, she was fading into the ashes,
But she was determined to rise again, her spirit battled.
She had a life still to live and a legacy to leave behind.
This was not her time to wither away and die,
Though her limbs ached and her body did not feel her own.
She struggled with adversity; she would not be beaten.
Each painful step was a testament to her strength of spirit,
Overcoming the trials and tribulations that life threw her way.
She did not give up or give in; quitting was not an option,
For she was a phoenix and was determined to rise again.
Through each and every struggle, she battled on,
For one day soon, the phoenix inside her would fly again.
As she triumphs over adversity, she becomes the fire inside her heart...

The Mermaid...

Take me with you beneath the waves.
Show me the magical world at the bottom of the sea.
Let me feel the water press against me like a second skin.
To dive to the depths with the creatures of the deep,
I will face my fears and conquer each one,
For I have put my trust in your love to keep me safe.
I have always feared the ocean; they call it aquaphobia,
But I no longer want to live in fear; I have been afraid too long.
Swim beside me, take my hand.
Help me live my dreams before we finally say our goodbyes...

Chasing After Love

He left her at the doorstep,
Heading for his next destination.
A part of him felt missing,
A part of her felt missing,
A spark had illuminated.
They both felt
Words were left unspoken,
But the feelings grew
Deep within.
The breeze blew on his face
As if bringing her first kiss with the wind.
The sun rays felt like her shadow chasing;
A yearning began
To touch her,
To feel her,
To taste her,
To kiss her.
Would she know the desire that was growing?
Did she feel the same passion for him?
He didn't have the courage to look behind.
He didn't have the courage to speak his mind.
He left her right there,
Allowing his feelings to subside,
For he was afraid of rejection...
She saw him walk away.

She felt his whisper in her ears,
"Come and find me, my love.
I'm nothing without you.
Stop me, now,
Before I go.
Express to me
That you feel the same as I do.
Come before it's too late.
Come before you just remember me as a beautiful memory
Not explored.
I want you now.
I want you forever.
Please, come and say
You want me."
She ran to him,
Held him from behind.
Before he could say anything,
She pulled him close
And kissed his lips,
Tasting him.
He pulled her close,
Ran his hands through her curves,
And without saying,
He said, "I love you,
Will you be mine forever?
For you are my destination,
And my search for my dreams ends here..."

Let The Rain Fall

The droplets of rain fell on her skin,
Soaking her to the bone.
She loved it when it rained.
It took her to another place.
She felt at peace in the rain;
Alive,
As if cleansed by falling tears.
The smell of petrichor hangs in the air.
All around, the air is sweet,
As if Mother Nature is smiling.
She bathes in the sunlight,
Dances in the raindrops.
She becomes the rainbow...

Lourdes Alexander

The Agony Of Distant Love

Being a sailor's wife gives me pride.
Life made him a sailor,
But God made me his life.
Life is not easy, though,
When the sea calls
And the life in me
Leaves with him.
The agony of being distant tortures my heart,
As I get to see him only once in a year.
I count the days while he is away.
When he is back, it seems like I'm in love all over, again and again.
We meet again like new lovers in Spring.
I shy away when he teases me with a wink.
I try not to blink.
I don't want to miss an instant
With each passionate hour.
I bloom like a Spring flower.
Loneliness had turned me into a withered flower,
But his love renews me.
I don't crave for the gifts he brings for me,
For I'm blessed with a perfect family.
They have taken me as a daughter and sister
And take the utmost care of me in his absence.
I always long for his presence, though;
Feel low when I need his embrace.
I silently endure the pain,
For I know he misses me too and endures the same.
From time to time,
We talk on the phone.
I can't send lovey-dovey messages.
They are scrutinized,
And I love him too much to embarrass him.
Often, I find myself on my knees, praying,
Knowing my prayers will cross the distance.
My prayers also comfort me.
They let me know he is with me even though far away...

You Are A Miracle

Don't fret if anything goes wrong in life.
There are lots of pages that are still blank in your life.
You have the pen
To write your own beautiful story.
Nothing can stop you
'Til you attain your glory.
Challenges come to make one stronger.
Tomorrow, you will understand
And tell your kin how you tackled them all.
God gave you a spirit that is courageous, my dear.
Don't forget that you are chosen
And blessed to be an Eve,
For she is phenomenal
And can weather any given storm.
Nothing can stop you.
Nothing will ever go wrong.
Your broken wings will be mended,
And soon you will soar high in the sky,
Achieving all your dreams
That you always wished for.
Remember, it's just a temporary phase,
So do not fret, my dear sis.
I believe this little storm in your life
Will miraculously pass by.

Make Me Believe

Love me tenderly,
Love me sweetly,
Love me like you never loved anyone before,
Make me believe that true love still exists.
Though my past has left a scar,
I refuse to turn bitter.
All I need from you is to make me believe
That my belief in love is tangible.
Heal my soul,
Fill the emptiness,
Make me complete
With your unconditional love.
Let me dive into love once again.
Let me taste it once again.

How I Love You

You
Are my everything.
I wish I could stop time,
Capture you
Within this heart of mine,
So not a second passes without you.
I'm so crazy about you,
Even as I lie sleeping
I am always dreaming
Of you.

You are my ecstasy,
My timeless melody.
You are the light of my life,
Diminishing darkness,
Making all things right.

You
Are the miracle in my life
Who makes my living worthwhile.
I love you with my everything,
And you know how I am feeling.
Forever in your arms
Is where I want to stay.
You are my angel
Who gets me through each day.
You keep my heart beating
With thoughts
Of you...

<u>Caged Bird</u>

She was on Cloud Nine.
She had found her soulmate.
She felt blessed to have him by her side;
The one who loved her,
Cared for her,
Treated her like a Queen,
Made her feel special
By loving her as she had dreamed.
She even thought of running away with him
To be his wife
'Til death would part them,
But life is never what it seems.
Destiny played a dirty trick,
For when she was lost in thoughts of him,
And living in her own world of fantasy,
He cheated on her.
It was a mere one-night stand
For him.
He felt no one would know
What happened in the darkness of the night,
But one night became a lifetime of responsibility.
His moment of weakness resulted in an unexpected pregnancy.
He was devastated,
For he loved his love.
He only wanted to be with his love.

He needed her to be his
For the rest of his life.
He felt he had wasted his chance,
Approached her,
Apologized for his unfaithfulness,
Pleaded for forgiveness,
And although devastated, herself,
She understood his plight,
Forgave him,
For she truly loved him.
The scar was deep,
But love is forgiving,
But she could not find it in her heart to be with him.
Love is forgiving.
Trust is not.
Though they both longed to be with each other,
The boundaries were set.
They shed silent tears,
And silently endured the pain,
Hoping like a caged bird
That their love would fly free.

Phenomenal Woman

You are a phenomenal woman,
Shrouded in humility,
Care, and simplicity
As you walk.
Men notice your curves,
Desire to touch that sensuous part
As it arouses secret desires in their hearts,
To hold you,
To draw you,
To pull you,
To sway with you
On the dance floor.
But
You seem to go unnoticed,
Even if you want to,
Because
You have a model's built,
Sexy and tall.
You are called that
Sometimes,
But your heart does not delight
In these names,
These so-called compliments
To your flesh.
All you need is love,
Not sex.
You are not a toy to be played.

You are beautiful,
You are sensuous,
Both tender and strong,
Irresistibly feminine,
And you long for a perfect man
To make you part of his,
Not just to be showcased,
Not just his beautiful wife,
But to understand
What lies in your heart.
This one will do anything for you
Without being told.
He surprises you,
Not with gifts,
But by being by your side,
Always.
When the need arises,
Who would feel empty and lonely
Without you.
Who would father your child
And make you a complete
Woman;
Not just his wife!!!
Who adores every part of you.
Your eyes drown him,
Luscious lips invite,
Your smile makes him crazy,
Your body seduces,
The feel of you arouses him,
Your breath lingers on his mind.
Without you, he feels lost.
He is the man
Your soul yearns to connect.
What you long for in a man,
Phenomenal Woman!

Silent Night

She was in a pensive mood
As she saw the raindrops on her window pane.
Memories of days spent with him,
Dancing in the rain,
Appeared before her eyes,
And she sobbed like a child.
Didn't realize why
He had left her without any reason,
Without a final 'Goodbye.'
She couldn't comprehend
It was a lie
When he had once said
He loved her.
She was his Queen,
His destiny.
She began to gather
Her torn heart,
But her heart ached.
Deep was the pain;
She could feel it
Running through her veins.
She ran toward the phone
To call him the last time.
He answered.
She choked
And couldn't utter a word.
He hung up instantly.
She tried yet again,
But all she heard was a busy tone.
She realized
He had dumped her then
Without a 'Goodbye,'
And all that he said
Was a pack of lies!!!

I Honestly Love You

I had tried to flee from this love thing
More than once,
But a darkness seems to cover me
When I'm alone.
Grief stings my heart.
The torture I go through each day is indescribable.
It seems like an old injury,
A wound that grows more painful each day.
Honestly, there's only one way to heal it,
For I know accepting you is the only remedy.
I try to resist,
Act stubborn,
Try to lock myself from this world,
From this ecstasy,
But your love keeps knocking at my heart's door,
Infecting the wound with pangs of love.
At times I even cursed the day I knew I loved you,
And always would,
And asked destiny why it had made me meet you,
Why my path crossed yours,
Why this soul of mine led my heart to you.
Can one change what is predestined?
I was destined to be yours before our births.
We were born to be together
And journey together through love.
I give up,
I surrender.
Quieten my stubbornness,
Allow your love to overtake me.
As me being honest with myself led me to you,
Instantly all wounds seem to have healed.
This moment I confess,
I honestly love you too.

If Not Here

I can't imagine a life without you,
My love.
I can't tread this journey on my own.
I need you to inspire me,
To comfort me,
To protect me,
To love me;
Your love defines me.
When I'm on my own,
Your shadow follows me.
I can see it even in your absence.
I hear your voice haunting me.
I see you in my dreams.
Where can I flee?
Is there any place on this Earth
Where love never exists?
For even in the war zone called life,
Nature exists,
And in Nature, love exists.
You have become my sole passion,
My prayer,
My destination;
I can't think of moving on.
If not here,
Our love will make it through
in Heaven.

Yearning For Your Presence

My Love,
Meet me by the starlit stream.
Your presence brings a glow
To my weary face.
You make me radiant,
Love overflows,
I can't get you out of my mind.
I feel you all around me
All the time.
Take me with you
To where the sky meets the earth
Like a lover.
Let's tread to that place,
Hand in hand.
Let's get lost in our own created wonderland.
Let's make a promise become true,
For I yearn to be right next to you.
Seasons may change,
Days might fly swiftly,
Life may even stand still,
But my love would ever be the same.
It won't wither
Or fall off like a dry leaf,
For my love has grown up with roots.
It will stay strong.
It can't be uprooted
By any wind or storm.
I live for you;
You alone, my love.
I know your heart
Longs to hear that,
So take me with you
To that horizon,
To our ultimate paradise...

Untold Flight

He left her without any reason.
She cried alone and wept all season.
He never felt the need to contact her.
She waited and didn't allow her fears to overpower her.
Days passed.
Gradually, she didn't shed any more tears
As her soul silently wept,
But her eyes didn't allow her to shed any teardrops.
She felt strong, although weak;
Wanted to shun life, but rather chose to live.
One day suddenly, he returned out of the blue.
He whispered, "My love, I missed you,
Love you,
And wanna hold you tight and kiss you..."
He confessed-
"Without you,
My days were lonely and sad.
I felt something missing,
Even though everything around was bliss.
I realized then,
What my heart had always longed for.
You are the one
That can fill this emptiness,
And it's you I want,
So let's give our love a second chance.
I want you to be always mine...
Let me hug you and feel your embrace
While you in turn can be filled with my fragrance..."

He stretched out his hands for an embrace.
She wanted to run and hold him tight,
But something stopped her.
She withdrew her steps,
Moved backwards instead.
She fled without a word,
This time.
She didn't give any reason
For her untold flight.
He froze there for a while.
That's when he realized.
A pain stung him so hard in his soul.
He understood the reason
Without being told.
He realized how he had once left her
While she pleaded for him to return.
He shed a tear.
Deep down he knew,
He had lost his love forever!

Musical Notes

Your love strikes
The perfect chord,
Enthralling my soul,
Igniting the passion
That I so blissfully had hidden.
As I submit to your love, unknowingly,
The musical notes fall clearly on my ears.
Its rhythm runs through my veins,
Making me dance like a ballet dancer
On tiptoe.
I feel surrounded
By the heavenly beings
As they dance with me
In unison.
Even when we are together,
In the crowd
I feel lost in your presence,
Lost in the melody of your love.
Neither do we need any choir,
Nor any orchestras
To play the tune
As our love plays the perfect romantic songs.
And you draw me closer to you,
Mesmerize me with your eyes,
And I forget where I stand,
Hypnotized in your spell
As a chill runs down my spine.
For you bend and kiss;
Feels like the first kiss,
Making this melody of love
A perfect romance...

Mending My Soul

Love, an awesome feeling
Has made me a dreamer,
Lost in a world of fantasy,
Dreaming away a dream
In which you are always there,
Smiling elegantly and coyly
As I think of you,
Glowing with beauty
When I see you,
Blooming like a flower,
Pure and unblemished,
Looking beautiful.
And the reason is you
That love touched me
When you walked
Through the trail of my broken heart,
Filling the emptiness.
I felt you deep inside.
Your love made me restore
My faith in togetherness
I had chosen to ignore
When I became yours.
I hardly realized
My cold, empty arms
Found something to hold.
The storms in my life
Began to slowly calm,
And all my burdens were swept away
As you showed me
How to weather the storms
That always scared me,
And into the golden sky
You carried me
Through it all
As we set free
To the very place
We were meant to be,
Where love is all over.

Remember Me

She blindfolded him with her scarf
And kissed him good-bye.
She asked him to remember her all his life;
Confessed she loved him
But couldn't stay.
Her ailment had overpowered her;
She'd only live for a month or so.
All she wanted was to live
In his memory as beautiful,
Even if she's no more.
So, she left him midway
Through this journey of love,
Wanted him to move on with another,
Even if a sword pierced her heart.
She took hasty steps,
And as swift as a wind,
Disappeared in the crowd.
He stood there, blindfolded for a while,
Breathing heavily.
In silence, he cried.
All pleas that he loved her
And wanted to be with her alone
Fell on deaf ears.
Nothing could stop her now.
She had made up her mind.
All that was left with him
Was the time invested on her,
The timeless memories
He'd cherish all his life.

No, he didn't blame her
But understood her stance.
He so wanted to be by her side
When death would embrace her.
She was right, he thought later.
Wouldn't it be difficult for him
To see his love die in his arms?
He untied the knot of the scarf on his eyes.
He stared at the pathway,
Visualizing how she might've walked by...

A Healing Love

She watched the dying embers
Burning radiantly in the fireplace,
Reminding her of the love she once had for him.
The dying flames,
Like the shifting embers,
Glowing then fading.
She watched the dying
Of the light
Turning into ashes.
She gathered all the ashes
Of her seared heart
And placed them in her soul.
If her heart were to love again,
It would have to be incubated in her soul
For a time.
She had no time for dying
Or having her spirit crushed to dust.
Hers was a defiant soul
That would never give up,
Do more living
Than surviving,
Believing
Love will live again,
Knock again
On her restored heart.
She still existed,
So love still existed
And would find its way to her.

Where there is love,
There is hope,
And she was full of love;
Love for all of life
But more for the love
Who loved her more
Than any others,
The love who would see
And treat her as a queen,
The love who would shower her with healing kisses;
Sweet, tender, and gentle,
Healing the scars,
Healing her heart,
Healing her spirit.
She desired to be healed.
She needed a healing love.

Priceless

The thought of losing you
Is not an option,
But sometimes it lingers on my mind,
Making me weary, soulful, and sick.

Just that one thought
Drives me insane.
My senses break down.
In seconds,
I feel lost,
Isolated,
Like a sharp sword
Piercing my heart.
The pain grows immense and intense.

Just the thought of losing you
Haunts me,
Tortures me,
Threatens me,
Teases me,
Weakens me.

I know I would never survive.
I know I would never be the same,
For I'm certain I would be completely destroyed.
I would want to die.
Just the thought of losing you
Is enough
To bring tears to my eyes.

There is no sorrow,
My love,
So deep as the thought of losing you,
For I feel depressed,
Sad,
Lonely,
Restless
As I wait to hear from you.
I'm wide awake.
My eyes don't seem to tire,
Even at dusk,
As my body beckons me to sleep.

Imagine,
If you can,
What you have done.
There will never be another.
No, there will never be another
Who will love me like you.

Yes,
I am afraid.
I feel empty within
At just the thought of losing you...

When Broken Pieces Come Together

I'm thankful to God,
Every morning and night,
For the moment you walked into my life
Was the moment I began
To love life.

I thank you for the respect you have shown,
And I thank you for the love you've bestowed;
So thankful that I feel I cannot express
From the depths and silence
Of my heart.

When I thought my journey through life had ended,
You opened my heart to a new horizon,
A new meaning,
A new love,
A new life.

As we came across
Into each other's lives,
Each with broken souls to deal with,
We both knew it was not mere chance.
Our destinies were different
From what the world thought they should be;
From what we thought they should be.
As we find blessings in the broken pieces of our lives,
We thank the Heavens for connecting us,
Adding love
And meaning
To our lives.

We met, you and I,
Not just to be part of each other's brokenness,
So let us write our story together
And give destiny
The sweetest revenge.

Ripping Into Pieces

The girl of his dreams lay next to him.
He loved her,
She loved him,
Wanted her to be his FOREVER,
But their love story was complicated
'Cause he wasn't ready to seal it with a covenant,
While she waited with hopes that one day he would surprise her
By proposing to her,
But the waiting seemed unending.
One day, she disappeared without informing,
Kept herself distant from his reach,
Not to make an end
Or seek another,
Even not to go through the ritual of questioning
Where this relationship would take its course.
That ripped her into pieces everyday,
For she had seen love in his eyes
That never lied,
And keeping distance would make him realize
What she truly meant for him...

For The Man I Love

You're the best thing that
Has ever come to me,
Nothing else in this world
Would I ever seek.
Your love is plentiful.
It's the only thing I would always need.
People say
Love is blind.
I have heard it,
But that's a lie, I know,
'Cause our love is certainly not blind
As we were destined to be for each other,
Even before we were born.
The moment our eyes met,
We had mutually interlinked.
Days and nights are not the same,
For without you,
My heart aches.
A mere signed document
Can never seal the covenant between us,
For the Heavens above have already
Sealed the covenant
By tying us together
In a perfect world.
Just you and I'd be there,
And you'd be all I ever needed.
I just want that world,
And I long for that life;
That love with you.
Take me to that perfect world, my love.
Make your pledges come true.
Let's rewrite our lives jointly
In that perfect world
Where our SOULS have already been tied to live in reality.
Yes, I desire that life,
That DIVINE LOVE with you forever by my side...

You're My Love and Life...

Ssshh! My Lady.
What have you been hiding
In that heart of yours....?
Can I gain entrance to your Soul, please?
Trust me, you can confide in me;
I won't let you down.
If sought, you have my shoulder to relax on.
I can take
All the pains away.
I know it's difficult for you to trust me,
An absolute stranger,
But I very well know
What it's felt like,
'Cause I too have once gone through that life.
I know how it hurts.
I can realize your pain.
Oh Girl, tell me what's wrong.
Don't forbid, please let me in.
The dark shadows can't steal your peace away.
Don't switch your heart on to lockdown mode.
Never....
You deserve a decent life,
'Cause you're LOVE,
'Cause you're LIFE.

To Render Eternity

They were strangers to each other
When destiny brought them together.
Out of the blue,
She knew
She could read his eyes,
Could feel him,
Saw through him,
Knew he had sold his soul,
Felt him losing himself.
His dreams were locked up in her,
His dignity gone.
She felt the pain in his eyes,
Knew he needed a friend,
Needed love,
And she cared for him.
She was there for him
Whenever he needed.
He'd lost his confidence,
So she uplifted him;
Had no thought for herself,
Not knowing if her love would be returned.
She gave him her all
And didn't realize
When he began to love her,
Nor when he became part of her.
She felt for his soul,
Gave him the love he needed
And kissed him,
Strong,
Wild,
Slow,
Easy,
With all her heart,
With all her soul.

She gave without measure,
Without thought,
Lost herself
Completely,
So that he might live.
His dreams became her own.
She was there
Through thick and thin.
When it came to her,
She could not be his.
He had his life,
So she restrained herself,
Slowly backing away.
Her soul cried out;
The emotions,
The connection,
The strain.
She'd helped him,
Removed the darkness that engulfed him,
Surrounded him,
And in return,
She embraced that darkness,
Without knowing.
Call it tragedy.
Call it love.
Without knowing,
She became his
Into eternity
And lived a life of emptiness.

Teach Me My Love

Will you help me forget my past?
Will you teach me how to live?
Will you teach me how to love?
Will you be mine,
Forever?
Can I entrust my heart to you?
Will you keep it safe, forever,
Like I have kept yours?
All I need is you;
Nothing matters to me.
I need nothing,
Just you
To be by my side,
Always...
To lift me when I'm down,
To hold me when I fall,
To touch my heart and soul,
To never let go of me,
To teach me what it feels like to be in love
And be loved,
For the shadows of my past
Follow me,
Haunt me,
Torture me,
Torment me,
Make me believe
There is no such thing as true love.
Say you will.
Yes, will you
Teach me to love, my love...?

Tears Of My Heart

I wish a wish,
If I could win back
The days we spent together.

I wish a wish,
If that time would
Never have come to an end.

You walked away
In silence.
I didn't look back.
I waited,
Hoping
You'd come back,
But you didn't turn back
Even once.
While I waited patiently,
You moved swiftly.

In my wildest dreams,
I never dreamed
You would move on.
I always believed
You would never erase me,
Not for a second,
Not from your heart and mind.
How wrong was I
In my assumptions...

Seemed like I never knew
The real you,
Even after spending
So many years with you.

I'm gathering
The broken pieces
Of my heart,
Trying to be strong,
Still cherishing the lovely moments
Spent with you.

Love is not a game.
If you lose,
You can't knock off the pieces
And play again.
Love is a promise
Never to say goodbye
As it's sealed forever in our hearts.

Lourdes Alexander

Sleep Inside My Soul

Tattered fragments of my heart,
Every scar was raw and fresh,
Every broken piece of my heart breaking into more pieces
As I tried to put them back together and gather myself.
My past
Chained me,
Haunted me,
Mocked at me,
Ripped me,
Stripped me,
Destroyed my sanity.
That's when my heart met yours.
You lifted my spirit,
Taught me to love
As if I had never been hurt.
You transformed every scar,
Every tear,
Every break
Into something more beautiful.
You brought back the smile on my face,
Which I seemed to have lost in this tempest of my life.
I needed tranquility,
I needed peace,
I needed to be loved like never before.
You seemed to have read my thoughts,
You seemed to have caught a glimpse of my pain,
'Cause you provoked me with your eyes
To lay my head on your bare chest and rest peacefully.
I fell for the love
I saw in your eyes;
Pure, radiant, and true.
Didn't realize
When I became submissive
And drew closer to you
'Cause you pulled me close,
Caressed me tenderly,
Played with my locks,
Hugged me gently.

I felt like a caterpillar
Nestled peacefully in its cocoon,
'Cause I connected with your heart and your soul instantly, my love.
I heard your soul whispering,
"Rest, my Baby,
I don't promise to you the moon and the stars.
I don't promise to you riches and treasures.
All I promise to you is my love,
For that's all that really matters.
I'm here.
I will always be there for you.
I will never let you go.
Sleep inside my soul;
There you will find the entire universe at your feet
Worshipping my Goddess.
You would be adored and desired forever.
My soul will be your dwelling place for eternity,
Even when this body turns to dust,
You will be locked inside there,
Forever.
What you have always longed for in this world,
You will find everything there;
Yes, tranquility, peace and love."
Suddenly, I woke up from my sleep
And raised my eyebrows to check on you.
I caught a glimpse of your face,
Found you sleeping peacefully,
But I knew deep down,
It was your soul
Which had comforted me
And did the talking,
For I whispered in your ears softly,
"Yes, my love,
I have indeed found eternal bliss,
And can now sleep inside your soul for eternity..."

Lost In Loving You

You are my life,
My soul,
My breath,
My existence,
My everything.
You will never understand
The extent of my love.
You are unaware
What misery I endure each day
To see you with another.
Life's journey without you seems incomplete.
I plead to the Almighty
To take away this pain,
To please take away this pain.

What a fool I am
To even make such a prayer,
For without you,
My life would be nothing;
Just a void
'Cause none can replace you.

No one.

So, even if we are not together,
I would rejoice in this pain.
I willingly accept
To silently endure this ache,
'Cause my heart doesn't know any other way to live.

Even if my love is unrequited,
My body,
My soul,
Both are no longer mine.

They were lost
The moment you walked through my life.
From then 'til now,
Until forever,
I'll be lost in loving you...

Lighting Up My Heart

You walked right through my heart
When my belief in love had almost fallen apart!
I felt your soul knocking on my heart's door
To let you in.
My mind reasoned out,
Go on lockdown mode;
Don't let him in!
I didn't realize you had the key,
For my soul gave you access instantly...

My mind played the devil's advocate and it said-
"It's a dream,
It can't be true.
You gotta be cautious,
So stop before you get hurt once again."
It made me doubt.
Oh, how I wanted to lock you out.
My heart didn't pay heed to its advice.
It whispered softly,
"He was sent from Heaven,
It's not a lie.
God sent him to rescue you,
Rescue him back,
For he is wounded too!"
All the reasoning seemed to have instantly failed
As I committed to you
Without thinking of the consequence.
I felt like you had stored all the love for me,
For your eyes did the talking
And set me free.
I felt drowned in your love.
I didn't have any more excuses.
Without thinking twice,
I gave you my breath, my Love!

Black and Blue

He persuades me it won't happen again,
Takes me closer and makes me believe
It was his drinks that had turned him into a beast.
Truth is,
He was totally sane
When he had beaten me black and blue.
It's his psychopathic nature
And temperament.
That's the truth of it.
Bruised and shattered,
Broken and torn,
That's how he leaves me
at 2.
No remorse or guilt he feels
As peacefully on the bed he sleeps.
I stay up all night.
In silence and in pain, I cry.
I can't even move an inch or two.
My spirit has been beaten black and blue.
One "bad" night
Became years of misery.
How I wish I could erase them
From my spirit.
Thinking about it
Brings back the hurt when I try to rewind.

The cruelty I had silently suffered,
A chill creeps down my spine.
I am tormented even now
When I look back.
How did I survive?
He made me a victim
In my own mind
For so long;
Black and blue.
But each time
My silent prayers
Were answered with a fist,
God saw my hands
Folded in prayer.
Yes, my spirit was black and blue,
But not my soul.
Guess what, I survived my fears,
I survived the tears,
I healed over the years.
I'm a black and blue survivor.

Paint My Life

Just when my whole world came crashing down,
You controlled my topsy-turvy ride,
Giving me the will to survive,
Exposed what was hidden in me;
My God-gifted talents.
That part of mine that was forgotten,
I felt this world was not meant for me,
Losing it completely.
I was so blindly in love,
Entrusting my heart to a heartless person
Who didn't deserve any part of mine.
In silence,
I shed many tears,
Mentally and physically tortured to the limits of sanity,
Embracing and nurturing all that hurt, I adopted it as my own,
Felt I was destined to live and not to live that miserable life.
I wanted an end to that life of mine.
I wanted to be missed and prayed for by loved ones,
Resting peacefully in their memories.
The Artist had not finished painting;
Only a black outline.
He hadn't mixed in beautiful colors.
That happened when He brought you into the picture.
You lifted the burdens of my heavy heart,
Healing my broken heart,
Showing me the different shades of love and life,
Making me believe
"The Artist" painted you
So that one day you could paint my life.

My Pen Refuses To Write

The nib breaks
Every time
That I change it.
It breaks.
It's mad.
There's no peace,
Only hatred,
Anger,
Envy,
Jealousy,
No courtesy,
No humanity
That exists throughout the land.
Atrocities on the poor
Always continue.
Damn!
The media leave it ignored;
It's not spicy.

The rich spend lavishly in bars and brothels,
Turning deaf ears to the cries,
The pleas
Of hunger-stricken children.
They continue
The blame game,
The media,
The politicians,
To prove who is leading,
Who is popular
Among the masses,
And whose story is true,
Plausible,
Believable.

How to forget
What the paparazzi do,
Covering up the rape victim's story
With sheets of paper
To gain popularity,
Stripping her more
Of her sanity
By writing that tiny story.
The cops and judges are equally to blame
For interrogating,
Demeaning
The victims
And not the criminals.
Law is blind, indeed,
For within no time at all,
Perpetrators are released
To devour more innocent lives.

Power, fame, and name
Are the keys to this game.
"Forget what's happening in this world!"
They say.
"That's not our fucking concern,
We party all night
With friends and family.
We stay happy.
We are tuned with ourselves."

Yes,
That's the reality
Of today's world.
I won't raise my voice;
I would rather ignore,
Pretend to be deaf,
Allow the injustice to continue
In this crazy world,
And my pen gets awfully mad
And refuses to write
Anything; I want to
Becoming nothing
Like me.

The Quest

(Collaboration by Salima Papillon and Lourdes Alexander)

(Salima Mansouri)

She threw the blame on life.
She thought she would get what she dreamed of
when she counted from one to five.
She forgot that she had to strive.
She forgot that she had to love to taste life.
She roamed in the world of fantasies to find the key to her happy life.
She sought for a realm to dwell in her dreamy life.
She forgot life would ask her to wake up to live and love.
Life hinted, "Love is Me."
She found the secret key to her happy life.
She LOVED, for Love was the only way to bring her to life.

(Lourdes Alexander)

She had beauty and brains too,
But her life was yet another Cinderella story.
She became mature at a tender age.
She accepted responsibility with a positive attitude.
She never let a day sweep by without a smile.
She cherished every moment of her life.
She believed that after every dusk there was dawn.
Her wings, though clipped, but her spirits were strong.
She weathered every storm that gave her a topsy-turvy ride;
Never gave up for she even defied life.
Life had to surrender and bow down at her unfailing spirit,
Turning into reality every dream she once wished.
Her story was hopeless, but she was a ray of hope.
She even got her love for she was love!

Sister in Heaven

I have a beautiful Angel up in Heaven
Who left me ten years ago.
I didn't get the time to bid her farewell.
I can't come to terms, even now that she's no more.

I wish I could talk to her.
There are so many things I want to say,
But I know she is smiling from above
And saying, "Sister, I'm here, and for you I often pray."

I miss her kiddie pranks.
I miss her sweet talks.
I miss the moments we shared.
I wish I could get her back.

I thank God for making her a part of me,
Although it was briefly,
'Cause she is still alive
In my memory.

Although she's in Heaven,
I know she is with me too,
For I can feel her singing,
"Sister I love you too..."

So, I blow kisses to Heaven,
To her every day.
Now she may seem far away,
But we'll surely meet again someday.

Quotes

He was blessed to create life through his art, while she was blessed to create life through her words. Creativity flowed within their veins. They both blended well to create a masterpiece called love, for they lived love.

She showed him the light while she embraced darkness. She showed him love while she embraced loneliness. She showed him the will to survive while she gladly embraced tears of joy... She never confessed her unrequited love 'cause she believed true love was selfless, and so she gladly sacrificed...

She became his anchor in his stormy sea of life. She moored him to the shore while she clasped the waves...

His heart bleeds words with such stirring lines that make her wonder as to who makes him craft such amazing lines. He honestly melts and touches hearts, spreading his light and showing what it is to be in love...

He asked her, "Would you love me the same way even when I grow old?" She said, "Forever, 'til death makes us part." It was her turn to stir his soul. She asked him, "Would you miss me if I died?" His honest confession stirred her soul, instead. He replied, "I would cry every day 'til life leaves me. I would carry you with me wherever I went." Her throat constricted, and unshed tears stung her eyes. His beautiful words illuminated a ray of hope in her dying soul. He had spoken his whole heart and mind that she was his precious treasure, his only possession.

He is among the dead, but love has not left him. He lifts his hand in prayer, praying for her happiness. He wants her to be happy, not sad. He wants to live in her memory as a beautiful dream, not as a painful one. All he cares about is her peace and joy!

He missed her like crazy. The thought of her brought a smile to his face. They were distant, but he thanked God for bringing her into his life. He loved the fact that there was someone special who cared, loved, and cherished him without reservation. He felt like his life was changing for the better the moment she walked into his life. She was his lucky charm. He couldn't imagine a life without her. She was no longer his need but his desire!

Her absence had created a void. He tried to fill the emptiness by being with another, but his heart and soul were no longer with him. He felt she would be jealous with this new love, but she was in no competition with anyone. She had her own charm and persona that no one could take away from her. He failed to realize that he had connected with a pure soul that he couldn't find in anyone else. No one. His soul would feel this emptiness forever!

She grew up reading a fairytale. She dreamed of living in a world where angels sang songs of love, but love seemed to be an obscure, faint echo in a crazy world that seemed unreal. Then, there he was. He had read the same stories. Her Prince Charming surprised her by recreating the scene of fairies and angels. So, he went down on one knee and proposed to her by asking if she was willing to become his Queen, forever. She blushed coyly and couldn't believe her dreams could be coming true. She nodded yes and bestowed him with a kiss with moist eyes. Her fairytale dream had come true, and they began living happily ever after.

He could see her love for him through her eyes.
He felt mesmerized by her eyes that could melt mountains.
He wanted to be held captive by those eyes forever.
He became sensitive and weak when it came to her love.
He melted. He felt his body and soul were no longer his
anymore, as they surely belonged to her. He wanted to
become worthy of her love. So, he thanked and promised
the Divine Artist to take good care of the blessing he had
found in her love. She was his Goddess.

She committed to him without thinking where her
destiny would take her. He seemed to be the perfect
man for her; her Prince Charming that she had read
about in her favorite love stories. She didn't expect
anything from him, just a lifetime of love. Her heart
seemed to have heard his soul speak words to her, which
his mind was reluctant to utter. She understood and didn't
listen to her mind. She therefore committed to him with a
promise never to say goodbye 'til death intervened.
She gave him her all without reservations.

They both believed in true love, but the scars of their past made them reluctant to connect with each other. They knew love was once again knocking at their heart's door, but they refused to open it. They didn't want to get devastated yet again, so they were extra cautious. Though they never gave up on love and life, they still decided to know each other better before committing to each other. Love had touched their souls. It bloomed and lingered in their memories.

She gives her perfect smile to the lady looking back at her in the mirror each morning. She believes in making a fresh start each day. She wipes away the past like a clean slate. She believes life is indeed a beautiful blessing. She lives Life. She is Life.

All she longed for was true love and a loyal partner, but as the days passed by, she came to realize that true love is scarce these days, and so is fidelity.

When she met him after a long wait, her joy turned into droplets of pearls which shed from her eyes. She was happy, but his love made her cry. She just expressed through her eyes that it was indeed the best moment of her life.

Never take her for granted. You never know what God has deposited in her life. She would be gone before you come back to your senses. You would then regret it for a lifetime. Why didn't you treasure her while she was with you?

You know you're in love when you want the best for that someone special and their happiness matters to you more than your own.

She saw the butterflies taking their flight.
She longed for wings to fly.
She longed to be in that place
Where they trade in love—
Nothing else.
But she became sad when the wind brushed her face,
Making her realize
That her wings were clipped.
She didn't have the right to dream.

Slowly, her feelings began to die. She no longer sheds any tear for him because she has come to realize that he is not worth her precious tears.

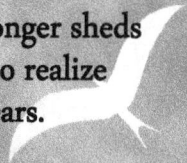

She knew that even if she got far away from him, he would live in her memory. She could never utter the word "Goodbye." The pain would linger within her for an eternity. She was prepared to live with it for eternity because she loved him with her entirety.

She sees him wherever she goes. He lingered in her heart and took her all. She chose to be silent. She got lost in her wonderland and didn't know how to control this feeling that intensified her days and nights. All that she wanted now was to be by his side, forever.

He needed someone to love him, even when he confessed all his flaws, to stick around and to hold on, and to never give up on him. He needed someone to lift him when his spirit was crushed and someone to be there for him when he had nothing but love to give. He needed a love that loves him wholeheartedly. He didn't need a perfect lover, because he knew her love was perfect for him in its imperfection...

Her dream agitated her to be awake, even when it's time to sleep. Nothing could stop her from achieving what she had already dreamt. She is never going to give up 'til she reached for the stars.

When lending alms, do not let your left hand know what your right hand is doing. Do not make the deprived feel that you are doing a huge favor for them. Remember, God has given you more so that you can share with the needy.

Everyone has a secret Angel who watches over them without their knowledge. Such souls only care about their well-being and want the best for them, even if it means caring from a distance.

There are times when some friends whom you counted upon have turned into foes. Your Master knows if they were wearing a mask of being a friend and fooling you. He knows their selfish motives. He knows who is best for you and who deserves to be by your side. He will therefore root them out from your life for your own safety. Trust in Him. He is protecting you from the evil souls.

She loved him but never confessed. She admired him from a distance. He was her breath, her life, but she was a soul who believed in suffering in silence, rather than losing his friendship forever.

His love brought out the best in her, and she sparkled
with different shades of light, expelling all the darkness
that had crippled her for ages...

Even when I'm in my deepest slumber,
I feel you cuddling me warmly.
I feel you imposing gentle kisses on my forehead, lips,
and deep down my spine.
I don't want to wake up from my sleep.
Want you just to do it, again and again.
I want to be in this spell forever,
and want to enjoy this moment eternally...

At times, it hurts that the good that you do goes
unappreciated. At times, people are ungrateful.
Don't worry. Continue doing the good work in silence.
Your Father is watching and jotting down all your good
deeds, and one day you will surely be rewarded.

You don't have to depend on anyone. Trust your instincts if
you have to make any important decision in life. Your spirit
will never lie to you 'cause God's spirit dwells within you.

When someone attacks your spirituality, do not be offended. Let go. Stay calm and composed. It simply means that you are one with the Divine. It's the Evil One who is trying to rebuke you and is shrouded in human form.

Just when she was about to stop believing in love, he came along, kissed her forehead, and made her believe that true love was not just a dream.

I asked God, "Is love for real?" He asked me to look into the mirror and made me realize that I was His greatest masterpiece.

She doesn't need a man with fake promises. She needs a man who will bring out the best in her and be there for her always, in good times and in bad. Someone who doesn't curse her but understands her and accepts her as she is.

There are times when you stop being nice to people who have shown you their true colors. These people would try to replace you. Don't let it affect you 'cause you are irreplaceable. Not everyone has a heart like yours. The problem doesn't lie in you but in them, 'cause such demons are on the hunt for souls who are weak and tenderhearted. They will use them 'til they squeeze out all the goodness and then forget that they stood by their side during their worst stages of their lives. Don't change yourself due to one bad experience, 'cause there are genuine souls who are really in need of help.

It's during the difficult trials of your life that the mask of fake friends falls off.

That she cannot conceive does not mean that she does not have not a mother's heart, a mother's care. She has been gifted with the love of life that is the essence of motherhood.

He saw that she was suffering within but was pretending that all was well with her. She bled her heart out through words. He was aware a poet is incomplete without love. So, he began to feed her heart and soul with his unconditional love. Beautiful words began to slowly sprout out from her heart. He rejuvenated her dying soul by showing droplets of his love on her, and the dying poet was reborn...

She is Air
That you can breathe.
She is Fire
That consumes you with passion.
She is Earth
That surrounds you.
She is Water
That you need to survive.
She is Clothed
In all the elements of nature.

She pledged to extract all the negativity from the past and focus on the good things that life had to offer, by living the life she had always imagined.

He surprised her by leaving his imprint on her with his gentle touch that was light, yet electrifying. She was always in control, but the deep rumble of his voice somehow touched her somewhere deep inside her as she moaned and ached for more. He couldn't resist and showered his fierce kisses upon her. And then he whispered in her ears, "You're mine, Baby, forever..."

When she shares her past or entrusts you with her heart and her wounds, she has entrusted her life, her broken pieces — her deepest part with you.
Do not break her trust; rather, safeguard her heart and her wounds as you would your own...

The pain would not let her speak, but her heart found a way to do some speaking in her poetry.

Nature lives within her, entwined in Divine beauty with all of nature. She is the seed that can grow into a beautiful forest, and every breath she takes is a new season of wonder. She is nature personified. She pulses with life.

She is the rhythm that tunes your life.

She hid all the secrets in her eyes.
She is a lady full of mystery.
You want to know her story?
Listen to what her eyes convey.
That's the doorway to her heart.
That's the doorway to her soul.
All her mysteries will unfold
When you learn the language of her eyes.

She is the light in your life that dispels all darkness.

She was born naked, and her soul is still naked.
Clothes are not going to shield her spirit, but the
love from a good man surely will.

She begins her day with the Creator. She believes God lives
within her. His love would never allow her to break or fall.

She had shielded her heart because she didn't want it to get hurt yet again, but the moment her soul touched his, she knew she belonged to him, so she gave freely without thinking twice.

The moment he left was the moment she began to miss him. She wanted him to be always by her side. He was all that she craved. No one could bring her the peace that his mere presence did...

She is not just your shadow. She has her own individuality; her own identity. She doesn't depend on a man for survival. She has the capability to do everything on her own. Don't try to overshadow her.

Stop thinking of situations which have not occurred. This will disrupt your life. You will dig your own grave by overthinking. Train your mind to inhale positive thoughts and flush out negativity from your system.

Do men cry?
Real men do cry. They cry when they are afraid of losing the love of their life. If a woman makes a man cry, that means she dwelt in his heart, mind, and soul, and he feels lifeless without her.

He prefers to be silent. He fears to break the silence and tell anyone about his plight 'cause society would believe her, not him. He doesn't want to become a laughing stock by confessing he was indeed abused.

She enjoys being herself. You will be able to catch a glimpse of her true self and her appealing beauty when she is in sync with nature.

Don't call her hot and sexy, but call her beautiful. That's what she longs to hear from the man she loves.

Tuck me gently under the sheets.
Whisper sweet nothingness in my ears,
And I will drift off to a new world,
Away from dreams...

All she wants is a good man who will love her forever, even
when she is no longer young and beautiful, and who
continues to treat her with respect and makes her believe
that she is the best thing that has ever happened to him.

...in silence, her heart cries, "If only he knew that
he meant the world to me?"

He guarded her dreams as she slept with his
innocence and chivalry...

With every "I love you," you stole a piece of me.

She is clothed in simplicity. No, she doesn't need camouflage makeup to cover her skin if it has birth defects. She is beautiful just the way she is.

Never comment that she is ugly due to her skin tone. She is beautiful, inside and out. She is divine.

She is Eve who gives herself completely - heart, mind, body, and soul to her Adam. Be the one whom she can always count on. Never take her for granted. Love her like she loves you. Treat her with dignity and respect, 'cause that's what she deserves and always longs for.

Take me to the place where the earth and the sky meet, for nature depicts love so perfectly in the stillness of the night.

She prefers to blend into darkness when she's about to break down, as she doesn't want anyone to empathize with her. She is a strong woman who knows how to emerge victoriously when faced with different challenges in life.

In my thoughts, you now dwell.
To whom should I tell my story?
Even if I try to erase you from my mind,
How can I erase you?
'Cause you flow in my blood
And are held captive in my heart and soul.

Although her past has crushed her sanity, it couldn't
crush her spirit 'cause she admires everything around
her that reminds her of love, hoping that someday she
would find her love once again.

I have fallen in love with you all over again.
My heart races at the mere mention of your name.
I realize now you never left me;
We just seemed to drift apart,
But there was always a part of you deep inside my heart.
Can true love last forever, can it truly be—
That I was meant for you, just as you were meant for me?
It feels like a dream, but for the first time I truly see—
This is how love is meant to be...

Life never goes according to plan, so expect the unexpected
and you will never be disappointed at the new things
you discover...

Love is like a flame that burns in two hearts,
separately — two burning hearts that burn as
one in the flames of their passion.

Love shouldn't be confined only within the four walls of
a room, 'cause nature joins in to celebrate love when two
hearts reciprocate their love openly...

When she is quiet, it always doesn't necessarily mean
that she is sad, but she is searching for some answers and
perhaps meditating. Let her be.

True lovers never look for physical beauty but rather
dig deep within each other's naked soul and accept
everything - the good and the bad, wholeheartedly,
'cause they believe love is not perfect.

Watch her eyes closely. If you see immense pain,
that's a sign that you haven't given her ample time. Make
time for her. Make her feel extra special each day, 'cause
you're the only one she cares about, and you're the only
one on her mind every night and day.

Two faces, two entities, two hearts, two souls, but when
in love, they lose their own individual identities as they
head together on a journey to be one face, one entity,
one heart, and one soul.

She loved to linger under the façade of a softly whispered
kiss that she once dreamed of. It felt so real. She didn't
want to face the reality that he was gone...

I want to live in a house made from paper,
So when I feel inspired to write, all I need is a pen.
I can write upon the walls, the stairs, and the floor—
All my feelings and thoughts when I think of you,
Of how I miss you so, the agony I feel inside,
Knowing you are not here in my paper house with me.
Your absence makes me cry; I weep words on paper.
My ink is blood that dons my paper walls as I write,
"I love you..."

Distances never matter since souls are often connected
and meet each other at night
when the rest of the world sleeps.

Love's touch is pure and divine.

While she sleeps, even nature creates a peaceful
environment for her.

He wanted to touch her but couldn't. Death had created
the distance, but death could never win, nor could it stop
love from loving, 'cause he had already secured a place
and dwelt in her soul, heart, and memory.

She has the power to rise and shine, spread out her
wings and scale unimaginable heights, even when
hope seems bleak, 'cause she is strong, although
she might appear weak.

The good and the bad both reside within you.
It's not in the world but within you. It's in your hands
whom you want to give more empowerment to.
The choice is ultimately yours.

Caress her feet. Don't make her feel that any part of her is
ugly. A true and perfect lover finds every part beautiful.

She is the Queen of your heart. Treat her with respect and
dignity. Pamper her. Love her. Surprise her. She deserves
all of it. Then, see how the Queen would submit and love
her King without any reservations, whatsoever.

Bask in her love to find the real meaning of love.

Do you want to see the different shades of life? You don't
have to roam anywhere around the world, 'cause she is
there right next to you, but you never understood her. She
plays so many different roles, effortlessly. She becomes your
mother, your wife, your lover, your daughter, your sister,
your teacher, your friend, and the list goes on.
She completes you. She is life.

She is an Angel. You can't see her wings, but you need to keep your eyes wide open to see the way she has loved you, cared for you, stood by you, and has never left you, even when the situation beckoned her to leave. She walks on this earth when she could have flown high up in the sky, 'cause she is a humbled soul who loves you without measure.

Silence has become her sole companion. You can't see her in pain, nor can you see her tears flow as her heart and soul cries from within. Love's magical touch has made her calm and composed, for now she waits patiently without complaining whenever she misses her love.
It's love that brought the change in her.

She met him for a reason. Not only was she going to heal him, but she in turn was going to be healed too of all her brokenness. God had brought them together for a purpose; to heal each other's wounds. And so, they became each other's smile.

She is like the Sun that rises each dawn to brighten your life.

She gave him her heart. The thought never occurred
to her if he would love her back the way she did.
Just a mere eye contact with him and she would glow,
'cause she knew love found her when his eyes met hers.

She woke up before sunrise and took a glance at the
handsome man lying next to her. She thanked the Divine
and believed he was a blessing sent from above. He was her
Prince Charming, her dream come true. She loved him
with all of her and became submissive like a devoted wife.
There was no space left within her to love anyone else, for
she knew he was the only soul who could complete her.

She closed her eyes, tried to sleep, but thoughts of him
lingered on. She could see him smiling back at her. She
wondered, why it was so difficult to erase him out of
her mind when he was the reason for shattering her
into pieces? That's when she realized that he had left her,
but she still loved him. It wasn't easy to let go, but she had
a life to live. So, she smiled at the good memories shared
with him, and that's when it was easy to let go of him....

Her smile makes his heart melt
and makes him forget his sorrows.

His voice soothes my soul. His care and concern make
me believe that I capture his thoughts, day and night.
His absence creates a void in my life, while his presence
makes the world around standstill. He is an elixir that
heals all my brokenness. I can't envision a life without him.

Sometimes, all she longs for is to lay her head on his
chest and cuddle in his arms. She loves it when he runs
his hands through her hair, pulls her closer, and hugs her
tightly. She loves to hear the tune of his heartbeat, and the
fragrance of his body soothes her soul. It feels
like Heaven in his sweet embrace.

Her past didn't allow her to move ahead, but Destiny had something in store. It unfolded a new chapter by bringing him into her life. She wanted to let go of the past, but a part of her stopped her. She felt like going back to her lost love and giving him a last chance. Her heart cried out, "Stop, don't repeat the same mistake. He was never yours. Look at the new-bloomed love that's waiting to embrace you." She closed her eyes to see whose she shall be. That's when she saw the new love smiling back at her. She chose him for eternity...

She intercedes for him in each and every prayer. He is a blessing sent from above. All she longs for is his love and respect 'til her soul leaves her body. He was her reason to live.

He is my piece of peace. His presence sparkles my dull day. His voice brings a glow and a smile to my face. His touch makes me feel wanted. He is my soul, and I am his soulmate.

He never believed in love. Her love ignited the fire in his soul. His love grew like a flame grows, and together they melted in passion.

Have you ever felt life playing chess with you?
Suddenly, you collide with someone, only to find
you can never be together.

She missed his gentle, pure, and divine touch. She
felt she was his world the moment he embraced her.
A chill ran down her spine. His touch worked like an
elixir, bringing her dead soul back to life. She felt safe
and comforted in his arms. His touch was his signature
he had written on her soul.

She stared at the sky, trying to lose the world. She only
wanted to see his face smiling back at her and feel his
warm embrace in the cool breeze. Suddenly, it began to
rain. She was brought back to face the reality that a
woman can easily get lost in a love that isn't real...

"I dreamt of you," she said.
"Really? What did I do?" he asked.
"You kissed my forehead and told me that you'd never let
me go, even if I made you mad," she said.
"That's not a dream, my love. You are my heartbeat.
I can't live without you." And he bent and gently
kissed her forehead.

The ink is her pain bleeding. Feeding the silence, she endures behind shut doors. The bleeding is her attempt to convey to the world the quiet misery of silence. The words are for others living in silent pain, as well. She wants them to know that misery has company...

It's easy to teach someone how to be when being in love. But, can someone teach someone how to stop loving when the other side of the love loves another?

She recreated the same scenario once again so that it triggered his memory that she was once his world. All she longed for was to be remembered in his thoughts...

She never told anyone what her dreams were. She dared to take one risk after another. Miracles often take time. She chased away any voice trying to stop her from pursuing her dreams by chasing her ideas. She dreamed of creating her own life.

He never told her he loved her. Whenever they met, he pulled her close, hugged her tightly, and without saying a single word, gently kissed her forehead. She understood what that kiss meant. It meant he cared for and respected her. He didn't want her to feel like an object for his sexual cravings. It meant he was there to be her comforter, her protector, and would come in-between her and anyone who tried to hurt her. He wanted his actions to profess his love. And so, they did.

Her eyes couldn't tell the same lies her lips did. She had repeated, over and over again, that she never had feelings for him, as if trying to convince herself more than him, but her eyes told him the truth of it. The proof of it was in how she looked at him...

Love crosses all borders that keep us apart. Our love will find a way to be together; I can feel it in my heart. 'Til then, the shadows of your love will keep me warm, for I can feel your presence coursing through my veins...

She loved him like crazy. She expressed it through her actions, but whenever she tried expressing it in words, she felt all choked up. And so, her love remained silent...

Even in his absence, she could feel his presence, since his scent lingered in the air. It felt as if she carried him everywhere, and her scent no longer existed.
She had lost her sense of self.

Her beautiful eyes put him into a trance. He drowned in her eyes as if they were a sea of stars, a galaxy of hopes. He loved this space and didn't want to turn his eyes back to the stark reality of a life without her eyes to look into, so he chose to remain lost in the moment...

She decided to let go and not to think of him anymore. The more she tried, the more her heart ached. It pined for his tender kiss and tight hugs. Life felt incomplete. She was miserable, pretending all was well with her. But slowly, she was heading towards self-destruction. She felt his love was her only hope for survival.

She chose to open up her life to a selected few.
Trust issues owned her thoughts.
No, she didn't have a bad attitude or prideful thoughts.
Her past had taken away her sanity,
Had demoralized her spirit,
So she sought light.
She sought truth.
She sought a purer light of love,
But still she found it difficult to open up.
The light she had known had betrayed her,
And trusting love had become a trust issue...

A relationship built on love is better
than the one built on barter...

He was her friend, her soulmate, her everything. All she
wanted was the best for him, even if it meant staying far
away from him. She somehow could never stop caring and
thinking about him since he was her dream come true.

She thought of him, missing him like crazy. She needed a lifetime with him, because she loved him beyond anything that could be measured, even time. But she refused to confess that, because she didn't know if she had a part in his future, and she did not want her dream to be crushed.

When colors merge, a vibrant beauty emerges...

Her heart was no longer hers,
For he became captive.
He too never wanted to flee
But wanted to be caged in it for eternity...

Once, he was her love. Then, he became her inner wound for the torture he inflicted on her heart, mind, body, and soul. She tried her best to forgive, forget, and start a new life again with him, but he wasn't the man who was supposed to journey in life with her, for he never really loved her the way she loved him. Days passed, and slowly her feelings began to die and she stopped crying for him. Slowly, it dawned that he was never meant for her and was the biggest mistake of her life. She forgot and forgave him. She let go of all the aches and hurts, for she needed to live in peace...

She awakened his soul and made him realize what love's touch meant. He touched her without touching her. It was the way he called out her name, the way he looked at her, and the way he paid heed to every little thing she uttered. He, in return, touched her soul deeply.
She had become his only addiction.

He painted the colors of rainbows in her life.
He taught her how to live,
and she taught him how to love...

She was mesmerized by the sensuous aura of perfume which he emanated. Even while she was alone, the fragrance held her captive, and she was lost in his love...

He felt she was just a friend, but he missed her even when he was with his love. He failed to realize that in friendship was hidden a true love, his love. When realization hit him hard that she was his shadow, it was too late. She had relocated. He felt her absence everywhere. An emptiness filled his heart. He wanted her back but didn't know where to find her. She was gone...

The rains flashed memories of the time spent with him. She felt his presence in the musty, barky smell of fresh rain...

When he saw her again, he began to reminisce about the good times spent with her, but she was no longer the loquacious girl that he used to know. She had changed over time. She had retreated into her shell as if a butterfly had climbed back to the safety of its cocoon. He smiled at her, but she walked away and disappeared into the distance like a faded dream...

True love sails through all adversities...

If love was so easily achievable, Shakespeare's *Romeo and Juliet* would not have been a tragedy...

His tears could be seen in her eyes. His smile could be seen on her face. His voice could be heard in her song. His dreams had become her vision. She was so entwined with him that she could read his thoughts even before he uttered them. Whenever she was asked what love meant to her, she blushed and said, "Love is he..."

True love does not come with rules and regulations. There is no set pattern to love, nor should there be. Love comes together like creativity and innovation. Love is a spark. Follow its light...

A butterfly doesn't listen to a caterpillar who tries to discourage it when it's going on through the process of metamorphosis. It endures the painful process and changes into a colorful butterfly, winging from one bud to another. We need to learn from this process and shouldn't fear the number of obstacles life throws into our path. It's a process, and soon we too will be winging like a butterfly...

She trembled when she found herself alone with him in the elevator. Her heart pounded in her chest; she smiled, then blushed. They were so in love, their eyes met in a stolen moment of togetherness.
This felt like the perfect moment to steal their first kiss. He pulled her close, bent in, and kissed her lips; it felt like pure bliss. Lost in the moment, time stood still, but the elevator took them higher.
Before they knew it, the elevator announced they had reached the floor. The magic of that first kiss was broken; they looked at each other and smiled...

Life threw plenty of curveballs at her. She faced all the adversities alone. No accusation or humiliation could stop her. She bounced back. She emerged victorious, to everyone's surprise. She's a fighter...

Don't be stressed about what tomorrow may bring. Treat each new day like a blank page, and write a brand new story...

He came home late at night and saw her sleeping peacefully. He so wanted to hug her and kiss her that very moment, as he had missed her all day. He realized then that she too must have been waiting for and wanting the same. Just then, he saw her smiling in her slumber. He felt perhaps she was already hugging him in her dreams. He blushed at the thought and slowly kissed her forehead. He spent the whole night watching her sleep...

She erased the painful memories that lacerated her mind. She believed in forgiving, so she cherished only the good times spent with him...

A beautiful soul can touch the lives of others by feeling for others without having any hidden agenda...

Assumptions without communication is the root cause of all problems...

Give selflessly and see the seeds sprout when
you least expect it...

She dances when she is down.
She hides her tears behind a smile.
She never uses anyone for her own selfish motives.
She lives a life of sacrifice...

She runs through the waves as the white horses
chase her down. She loves the feel of the water
on her feet as it soothes her, allowing her to be
wild, yet be at peace like the sea...

Infuse positivity into your veins when you are aching
in pain. See? The anguish vanishes as you begin to
feel as fresh as a new day...

Love is an elixir.
It cures life when it is not feeling well...

Unforgiveness is a poisonous toxin. It will consume you
slowly. Release the toxin and heal yourself...

When the breeze gently kisses my face, it takes me on a
journey. I am blown back down memory lane
and straight into your arms...

You'll know my love for you is very special, because though
I no longer live, I know a little piece of me is alive in your
heart. Though I faded like a shadow, I hope the sun will
always shine for you. Even through this great distance,
I can still feel your kiss as it lingers on my lips. Your
loving embrace still keeps me warm. I can feel you with
me on the breeze. I never left you, and I never will...

Adam only truly became the first man
when God created Eve...

She chose loneliness over betrayal...

Love is not fake. The one who preaches love doesn't necessarily know the meaning of true love. Beware of fake words and false promises...

Just because she loves you and gives you time to get your act together, don't misuse her trust and treat her like a fool. She will soon be gone before you realize it...

Practice patience before jumping to conclusions, for conclusions have no safety net, and the truth can often hurt...

Vows taken in love and marriage are usually forgotten with time. It's easy to utter "I Do" but in real life and once the journey begins, couples realize that the beautiful promises are not easily kept. One needs to realize that marriage is not a compromise or a sacrifice. It is a bond made from love...

Our coffee cups reflect our love.
You are dark and strong.
I am the spoonful of sugar.
Mixed together, our coffee tastes so sweet...

She showed him the different shades of love.
His dark heart was not willing to accept it because
his past had left a black hole in his soul that let no
light escape. Love, for him, was no more than a game
of winners and losers. She understood that. Still, she
saw a light in him. She began to follow him like a
shadow, embracing all the darkness and accentuating
his light. She saved him by becoming his shadow...

The scent of her body lingered like a perfumed memory.
He breathed in deeply and smiled as he thought of her.
Though they were apart, distance didn't seem to matter
as they had shared a piece of each other's hearts.
When he thought of her, he felt that she was still near him.
She was in the bird song and in the falling drops of rain.
He saw beauty now in everyday things as he missed her
every day.
Lost in her love, he felt content, and it changed the beast in
him back into a man,
for he had tasted love...

Whenever his eyes met hers, he breathed life into his paintings. The images he painted with words were no longer silent poetry for his fans to see; they became feelings that could be seen. She was his muse who inspired him to play with the colors of love and recreate life in verse...

Words are mere words if the poetry doesn't speak with passion and stir the heart and soul like love does...

She scribbled romantic poetic lines all over his body as he made love to her. He was her perfect muse, for she became a poet yet again...

Life should not be a synonym to the mundane. Rather, it should be lived with a certain panache...

Where you lead, I will follow.
You have swept me off my feet.
With you, I feel complete,
So take me along,
Wherever you go;
That's all I ask of you...

She chose to be subservient in love; she wanted her man
to be awakened, to stir the most masculine yet tender side
of his character. She knew it would bring out more passion,
more strength, more love. In building a lifetime together,
she only had to see the love and passion in his eyes...

She sits boldly, yet candidly, so enticingly she
looks at him with a shushhh on her lips...

If tomorrow I should die,
As a droplet,
I will live in your eye.

You'd lose me
If you'd shed a tear.

So, let me live there
In the pain of your soul, my love.

'Til we eventually fall into eternity,
One whole drop of love's rain...

It felt like Nature had created a perfect and romantic moment for them. He took her by the hand. Staring into her eyes, he slowly bent to her and whispered these words after a tender kiss, "Let me take the lead and show you the depth of my love, my Baby. You are the one my heart desires. You are the one that sets my soul on fire. You are the one I want to grow old with. Yes, you are the only one. None can replace you. No one..."

Let the life in you not die before the final curtain drops. Don't be hard on yourself when things don't go as per your plans. Relax. Breathe. Life has not come to an end yet. You still have to touch lives and leave your imprints before you sleep...

To hurt others is very easy. Try to love and be loved; it has its own charm...

She was a specific type of book, open yet closed for all but one. An untold story yet to be read... unreadable except by one...

<u>Acknowledgements</u>

Primarily I want to begin by thanking my Jesus, my Valentine, without whom my life is nothing. Praise you always for all the talents you have bestowed me with.

A vision comes to fruition not just by a visionary. There are many people who encourage and support you in making that vision a reality. When I never even envisioned that I could become a poetess or even have a book published, it was already a dream my mom had hoped and prayed for; her daughter's book to hit the shelves. There were lots of procrastinations and delays, but she kept on persuading me to have it published, and I'm glad that I would finally be able to place her dream in her hands.

I owe a big thank you to my mom, Catherine Alexander. I might not have been a good daughter, but I can't fathom a life without you.

To my dad, my handsome brother Joseph, my beautiful sister-in-law Suzanne, my aunts Elizabeth and Maria, my cousins Christie, Andrew, Fatima, Harry, Jennifer, nephew's hunk Clement and mischievous Zachy boy and my adorable niece Sophia, you have been an encouragement and light in my pain. Thank you for being there for me and helping me to realize that your love has always been a constant companion to me, as well.

A special thank you to all my mentors - Sir Madan V. Shakunta, Lawrence Parent, Ricky Cochran, and Paul Griffiths who helped me in my literary journey with your valuable suggestions and teachings.

I know people generally have one or two close friends, but by God's grace, I'm blessed with many. It won't be possible to list them all, but you do know who you are and how you have impacted my life with your uplifting words when my spirit failed.

The ones who share my deepest secrets and with whom I am in constant touch are my besties, Tania P. Santan, and Tania F. How can I forget Peter, Milfred, Bro Freddy, Bro Ronald, Sabrina, Rajitha, and Kalpana who too kept on boosting my spirit when I felt I wasn't a good writer and should

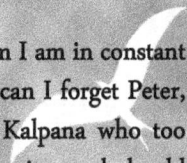

have called it quits. You have been a support system in all the ups and downs in my life.

A big thank you to my Spiritual Directors - Fr. Aniceto, Fr. Sanjeev, Fr. Gerard, Fr. Anthony, and Fr. Rui for molding me spiritually.

To my editor and publisher, Selina Ahnert, who extended all the help and support to make this dream a reality in the nick of time, a big thank you, sweetie.

I want to give an extra thank you to my brother, Joseph Alexander, for coming to the rescue and providing funds to help make this vision a reality. Thank you so much for believing in me. You are an angel.

Mom Laxmi Rajani came to my rescue while I didn't get time to proof read my manuscripts. I am indebted to her for taking her precious time out to spot the errors that I overlooked due to oversight. Thank you for being my eagle's eyes, Mom.

Last but certainly not the least, the man who wants to chase God with me, who loves to be behind the scenes and my soul cries out - "I have found the one whom my soul loves" -(Song of Solomon 3:4), a newfound love, Rohit Rajani, who came when I had lost all hope in life and love. Baby, you made my dream your dream, and you channeled and encouraged me to have the book published with all your efforts by firstly building a beautiful website. I don't have enough words to express my gratitude. Love you with all of me...

About The Author

What started as a hobby in poetry is now a way of life for Lourdes Alexander. Through her words, she expresses a myriad of feelings that are related to us all. With the touch of love, her pen glides across the paper, bringing her thoughts to life.

As she reflects on her journey thus far, from past struggles she has fought against adversity that has made her the independent woman she is today. Like a bird released from a cage, Lourdes is now unstoppable, and her imagination takes her wherever she wants to go. From shattered dreams to new hope, she writes from within the fathoms of her heart.

On a trip to Jerusalem, she discovered what truly matters most in her life. Having her unending faith in God and trusting in others, she stepped out of the shadows and came into the light. Lourdes' poetry goes beyond words. It is an extension of herself. Through her poetry, we understand her and learn about ourselves.

Lourdes lives in Mumbai, India, a big city in a small world. She loves spending time with her loving family and friends. She is a poet on the rise.

To see more from the Author, please visit her website and other social media accounts.

Facebook:
Search for Lourdes Alexander

Website:
https://www.lourdesalexander.com

Instagram:
lourdes.alexander

www.ingramcontent.com/pod-product-compliance
Lightning Source LLC
Chambersburg PA
CBHW031546040426
42452CB00006B/213